OUR JOURNEY
THROUGH
SHATTERED FAITH

Mike Newton

ISBN 978-1-64140-760-1 (paperback)
ISBN 978-1-64140-761-8 (digital)

Christian Faith Publishing, Inc.
832 Park Avenue
Meadville, PA 16335
www.christianfaithpublishing.com

Printed in the United States of America

I started writing this book early in the morning following my daughter's death not knowing or imagining what our future would be. I know many families suffer tragedies. I decided to finish this book after 10220 days from my daughter's death and future tragedies in order to help families and individuals with their sufferings in their lives. They say that after the loss of a child 75% of marriages don't make it. I hope from this book you will see the cause and how to correct that cause. I also wrote it to show people that god is the same today, tomorrow and in the future. We tend to lose track of ourselves after unimaginable losses. This book took rivers of tears and didn't come together without the lessons that were taught to me and remembered from my deceased children. This journey took me through my shattered faith and the road back. I hope people will read and understand that the shattered heart and mind can be healed to a degree that will not forget the past, but find a brighter future.

CONTENTS

Happenings in Our Lives

DJ's father died: December 3, 1988 (Lori's birthday)

Lori killed: February 22, 1989 (our daughter)

A friend's wife murdered: November 17, 1999

Twins born: November 17, 1999

Shaina (our granddaughter) ran over: 2002 (survival a miracle)

David (our grandson) born) February 23, 2004

My dad died: July 03, 2004

My mother died: January 26, 2006

DJ's family started feuding over the estate of her mother before she died. They took her to a nursing home in Sioux Falls, South Dakota.

Ken Huber, a friend and neighbor, killed his wife while she was in bed with her daughter: 2007 (DCI made a command center in our shop)

Michael Todd Newton (our only son) found out he had terminal cancer: September of 2009.

The Journey Through
Shattered Faith
Lorinda Lynn
and
Michael Todd
Moments
and
Memories of a Father

FOREWORD

I just finished reading *Tuesdays with Morrie*. I would highly recommend this book. When I finished, I felt compelled to write this letter. I wrote it to share my thoughts (which I am not very good at doing), but I wanted my high-school football coach to know that he played an integral part in my life and kept me going through the events in this book. When I was in grade school and through my junior year of school, I was forced to work harder than I really wanted to, chewed out for doing my own thing, ran to death in track (at least I thought I was at the time). I was put into positions I really didn't think I had the skills for, sometimes I did and sometimes I didn't. I had a coach that "believed in the kids" and always thought that they could do more than what they thought they could do. There are a lot of stories I could tell, but one that stands out in my mind and still does today is probably long forgotten in his mind. I can say that this incidence that took place between Coach Bride and myself has propelled me more times in life than I can count.

We were at a track meet in Pierre, South Dakota. I had only one event in the meet. I was a pole vaulter. Coach thought I should do more than one event, so he had me run the open half-mile. A friend of mine and classmate was the state champion in the mile and half-mile. Denny told me just to keep up with him, and I would be fine. Right, I was supposed to stay side by side with the state champion. I was able to stay with him the first quarter, but I knew by the time he kicked into high gear, I would be left in the dust. I told Denny that

I was going to fake a side ache and drop out because I surely didn't want to do this the rest of my high school days. Denny tried to talk me out of it, but I did what I wanted one more time. I faked a side ache and fell over in the grass. I saw Coach Bride come running over, thinking he was really going to be concerned. I was shocked and surprised when he reached me and kicked me right square in my butt. He shouted, "You're faking. Get up. You better get ready 'cause you are going to run on the two-mile relay team."

How could I have been so stupid? Now I had to run because other people are depending on me. What a lesson, and today, I thank Coach Bride for doing this for me. He taught me a valuable lesson. When things get tough as they always will, you need to pick yourself up and do what you don't think is possible. I have always admired Coach Bride and his wife, Jeannie. They have helped a ton of kids and raised some fine children. I have thought of this incident in some of the darkest hours of our lives. When we were knocked to our knees with the loss of two children, almost losing a granddaughter, having a grandson with seizures, losing two friends for murdering their wives, going through their trials for over two years, and losing my wife's family over greed. I can still see Coach running across the field with fire in his eyes. I can still feel his foot cracking my backside and telling me to get up and get going. After reading *Tuesdays with Morrie*, I felt it absolutely necessary to let people know how much they have meant to me in my life. There are too many to name, but I would like to name a couple. Carol Ann Baloun who helped me go with my wife of fifty years; when we were in high school, she taught me how to dance so I felt like I could ask my wife on a date. Mike Ferris has been a lifelong close friend, William Millar, Rich Baloun, just to name a very few.

When I was in the seventh grade, I worked at a cream station, and on Saturday nights, farmers would bring their cream and eggs to town in five- to twenty-five-gallon cream cans and their eggs in twelve- to thirty-dozen cases and sell them to us so they could buy groceries. I would test the cream for fat content and test the eggs to see if they were fit for human consumption. Then I would dump the cream into a big tank and clean the cans so they would be ready for the farmers to use again. When done with that, then I would write the checks out so they could buy their groceries. I did all this while my boss was across the alley, playing cards at the pool hall. I enjoyed working there because most of the time, I was my own boss. One day, I had to take some chicken feed to one of our clients who was a city farmer. As I pulled up to his house with the pickup, I could see a man lying on his back next to the wooden sidewalk. I approached him and saw it was our client all sprawled out, looking like he wasn't moving. I thought he was dead! I hurried back to the cream station and told my boss (who was in his sixties). He asked me if I checked him to see if he was breathing. I was thirteen years old and had never seen a dead person before. I said no. He told me to go back over there and check to see if he was breathing. I was scared to death myself, and I guess my boss must have been as well because he sure wasn't going to go do it. When I pulled the pickup back at his place, I could see that he was still in the same position I had left him. As I started walking slowly toward him, I noticed our town doctor turning the corner. I ran out and flagged him down. I told him what I saw and what was happening. He jumped from his car and ran over and checked him. Lucky for me, he came along. He told me that he in fact had died. I have never forgotten that event in my life. Since then, I have experienced several of those same events in my life. Life in a small town, you experience and see things that you would normally never see in a larger community. All of these happenings have helped me with the larger tragedies in our lives.

WE DIDN'T WANT TO
GO THROUGH THIS!

The date was December 3, 1988. Our three older daughters were in Sioux Falls, South Dakota, shopping and taking our oldest daughter out for her nineteenth birthday. The call came about 2:45 a.m.; the ring broke the silence of the night, like a thousand bells going off next to your head. It is always frightful when a call comes at that time of the morning. It was for my wife. St. Mary's hospital in Pierre. They wanted to tell her that if she wanted to see her father alive, she needed to get there as quick as she could. We quickly dressed and got on the road to the hospital, which was fifty miles away. With no traffic on the road, I did exceed the speed limit. Wouldn't you know the only car on the road at this time of the morning was a highway patrolman? We told him what we were doing. All he said was to slow down when we got to the city. It only took us thirty minutes to get there. The nurses told us we were minutes too late. We said our goodbyes and then tried to comfort Grandma. Then we had to call all the siblings and our children to tell them that their dad and grandfather had passed away. Our daughters got there early in the morning. The hospital had cleaned him up and left him there so his children and grandchildren could say their goodbyes. It was our daughter Lori's birthday. Lori had left college to come home and help Grandma take care of her grandfather. He had terminal cancer, which moved to his bones. He was in terrible pain every time he moved a small amount. She became very close to him in the short months that she helped take care of him. She watched him go from a 260-pound rough farmer and rancher to less than a 100 pounds at the time of his death. He always told me, "Mike, don't ever lose weight 'cause when you get sick, then you will have some to lose."

One day, I took him for a ride around the farm. He enjoyed showing me what he was doing. When we got back to the house, he opened the pickup door and slid out, missing the running boards, lightly hitting the ground. The sounds that came out of his mouth I will never forget. I have never as of this day ever heard an animal make these kind of sounds. He must have broken bones when he hit the ground.

One day, he called my wife and me into his room about a week before he died. He wanted to tell us something. He said that we had to be brave. We said, "No, you have to be brave. We will be fine, and we will take care of Grandma."

He shook his head and told us that we did not understand what he was trying to tell us. He told us, "You don't know what I am seeing. I am seeing three grandkids, and I will take care of them. There is a fourth, and I will take care of that one as well. So you have to be brave."

We said, "No problem," not having any idea what he was talking about.

He had lost three grandkids earlier in life. His son lost a child at the age of three to cancer and two died at birth; we had no idea where the fourth one was coming from. A couple of months after Lori's death, we thought back on what he was saying and realized that he had seen a vision of our daughter's death.

Prelude

The following is a heartfelt writing of the moments and feelings surrounding our daughter's death. It is written as a release of unbearable pain and emotions with an inner promise that Lori's presence will never depart from our lives. It is written with a thought of chronological order and of each and every person who came to share, and to love, and to hurt with us. I feel the need to express our deep appreciation to each of them.

Even though I told the deputy sheriff he just couldn't come into our house and tell me "Lori is dead," he very carefully called our family to help. Our brother-in-law and my sister brought my mother and came right away. My brother and his wife came. My cousin's daughter came and began coffee and did dishes. My sister and her husband drove from a town sixty miles away and stayed with us the night they were here to attend to people that we had no idea would show up. A good friend and one of the firemen that had to take care of Lori stayed into the night. The sheriff came to spend time, even though at the time, we did not understand the emotional trauma that he and the ambulance crew had gone through taking care of our daughter's body.

Our minister came from Pierre to support us and came to the funeral home to share our time with Lori. We were there to hug her, to pray, to love her, and to say goodbye to a body yet so beautiful, so warm, and so still! During the days that followed, time stood still, our hearts wept, our bodies were broken and had no feelings as though we didn't exist. So many people took over the chores I so constantly do every day.

Thank you! Thank you to Mike's sisters for being with me on the day of my dad's farm sale; the family was all at the sale. The selling of the farm equipment had seemed like a real emotional project before but not anymore. The machinery, trucks, and the tractors were merely objects with no feelings. The real emotion is the love and closeness in the memory of a father, grandfather, and now daughter.

The morning following the funeral was indescribably lonesome: the family gone, the children went back to school, Brenda for only a while. Lori would have been there to be with me now to talk, do my hair, help with the morning chores, and oh, how could we go on? As though they knew, my sister her husband and my mom came over. They stayed, sat, talked, and made the meals. They came daily until they went home to Seattle the following week. Our brother-in-law came and sat, never said much, but his presence was appreciated. He helped.

As though they knew we still couldn't sort out our feelings or hold back our tears from pain, family and friends came by. Thank you. Your cards of sympathy and caring continued for more than two months, and we looked forward to each word of Lori and your caring.

Although over two months have passed, our emotional time has stood still, and our very being is numb with loss and pain. Now though, we can come to you for help and strength because you so lovingly and abundantly came to us. Thank you to all family and friends.

Donna Jean Newton
A Loving Mother

LORI 88

The alarm clock radio came on at 5:30 a.m. It was really too early to get up, but nevertheless, the day had begun. I showered and shaved. I had to drive to Mitchell today for an all-day meeting and had decided not to stay over. I made an appointment back in Wessington Springs on the way home. The appointment was with an elderly couple. I remember driving into their yard, and thought how tragic it was to have worked as hard as these people must have all their life and ended living in a rundown shack like this. The man met me at the door; he was in his early seventies. He looked pale and unshaven. I didn't really know what they wanted. The house was neat despite the aged furniture. I liked this couple. They told me their story of how they had tried to get insurance but kept getting turned down because he was a manic depressant and had been for several years. I wanted to reach out to them and tell them I could get them whatever they needed. I wanted to say, "Hey, I can get you the insurance, don't worry," but I knew better. Our underwriters don't work from sympathy; they only work from facts, and he would never qualify for any insurance under the circumstances.

After I left to go home, I thought about my wife and daughter, Brenda. They had gone to Huron today to get Brenda's braces taken off her teeth. I thought I should surprise them and drive through Huron and meet them for supper. Then I thought, *What if I miss them?* so I drove on home. My thoughts turned to Lori and how she was doing on her chemistry test that evening, and did she get the job she applied for at Capital Motors in Pierre. Then I thought about Todd and how he was doing in college in Fargo. God, I thought I left so early this morning I didn't even say goodbye to any of my kids 'cause they weren't up yet.

Arriving at home, Hugo, our foreign exchange student, was studying at the kitchen table. Not wanting to make a mess in the kitchen, I said, "Hey, let's go out and get a bowl of soup. I have to be at church at 7 for Bible study."

We had a leisurely supper and visited about nothing. After supper, I went home and picked up DJ and rushed to church. It was my turn to do something for Bible study. For lack of time to put something together, I decided to play one of my favorite tapes I had been listening too. I heard this tape by Ann Kemial for the fiftieth time but always heard something new every time.

"If you hold your hands out and open them up and say, 'Lord, I'm yours,' whatever you want me to do, I'll say, 'Yes, Lord.' You can take out of my hands whatever you want or you can put into my hands whatever you want. I'll say, 'Yes, Lord,' to whatever you ask."

These words hit me especially hard this evening. After church, we went over to Grandma's house and watched some old home videos that had been transposed on a VCR. Going home about 10:30, we saw the local police and sheriff heading south out of town. I told my wife we should see where they are going in such a hurry but decided against that. I remember going in the house and instantly going to Lori's room to see how she did today. Then going downstairs to see if she was down there. Someone told me she had gotten home, and she and her boyfriend were going to go for a quick ride to his brother's and would be home shortly. I would go to bed, and she would bounce in when she came home to tell me about her test and about her day, sitting on the arm of the couch next to the bed talking all the time. I would say, "Lori, go to bed, I'm tired."

She would just say, "Oh, Dad," and keep on talking.

I was getting ready for bed when the doorbell rang. Nobody rings the front doorbell 11:00 at night. I put my jogging suit on and ascended the steps. My wife had already opened the door. When she opened the door, I heard, "Oh my god."

The deputy sheriff stepped in, followed by two people from the ambulance crew. I heard him say, "We have some really bad news. Lori is dead."

My wife screamed at him and told him, "You are lying."

More shock. I stumbled to the chair with tears in my eyes and my body going numb. I couldn't hear what went on the next few minutes. Disbelief went through my mind for several minutes. This is not true. What are they doing here, telling this to us? Then I heard Brenda scream and fall to her knees in horror and shock. Why are these guys in our living room at this time of night? Why are they telling us this? She just left the house not over an hour ago. Wave upon wave of shock went through my body. Then more people showed up from the ambulance crew.

"How?" my wife managed to ask.

She was shot in the head with a shotgun by her boyfriend. Her boyfriend had picked her up, and they were going to his brother's house. They said that he saw a coyote and was going to shoot the coyote. He pulled a shotgun from between the bucket seats and jumped from the pickup, and the gun went off, shooting my daughter in the head. (Why was the damn gun loaded in the first place?) He said when his feet hit the ground, the gun bounced off the seat and discharged into the back of Lori's head. (Why was the gun loaded?)

Her boyfriend entered the room supported by his two older brothers. He collapsed into my arms with jerking sobs. All I could think about was *Why was the gun loaded?* Then all he could say was "I am sorry, I'm sorry, I'm sorry."

I looked at my wife, and she looked back at me. Without saying a word, we knew what we had to do. We had to ask the Lord to forgive him, and we had to forgive him. This was probably the hardest thing I had ever done in my life, but we did it without reservations. Nothing was making any sense at this point.

He was going into shock. The ambulance crew was at our house. The crew urged his family to take him to the hospital. He was almost in a convulsive state. After the ambulance left, people started showing up. Where had they come from? Who called them? It was past midnight.

Dazed, confused, numb with shock, we sat and talked for a long time. The funeral director, a friend of ours, came to the house. We broke down again when we saw him. Not wanting to see him but needing to know if they were lying to us, we needed to see Lori for ourselves. We went to the funeral home. Entering the embalming room was rough, to say the least, on both my wife and me. We never had to do anything like this before in our lifetime. When we entered, there lay our beautiful grown daughter. She had her black leather letter jacket given to her by her uncle, borrowed earrings from her sister, a stolen scarf from me, her Isotoner gloves given to her by her boyfriend, jeans, and tennis shoes. It was real! God, I didn't want it to be real. I didn't want to leave her. (Why was that damn gun loaded?) She was our queen, our baby, our child that turned into a woman. She had taken her chemistry test that evening and passed, been told she got the job in Pierre at Capitol Motors, and told me the day before that everything between her and her boyfriend was terrific. Dreams were shattered, lives were shattered and our faith, was shattered. Lives would never be the same. Why was God doing this to our family? Hadn't her boyfriend gone through enough? His mother died at an early age, his father died in a plane crash, his dog was killed, and his horse died. How much of a test does God want to put on a human being? Why? Why? Why? Had we done something wrong? What had we done that God didn't like? We had been faithful and grown our kids up in the church. I hate God! He doesn't like me either! Everything that I was brought up to believe was wrong, all lies, all lies. Through all of these thoughts and tears, I realized that we have to remain strong for our other kids. Oh my god, we have to tell our little girls. We have to call our son at college. We have to wake Hugo, our foreign exchange student, and tell him. What do we do now? After waking and telling the little girls and calling our son, Todd, we spent time consoling and talking and crying with each child. We went to lay down and tried to get some sleep, but sleep would not come, only stirring, talking, and crying. Finally, not being able to sleep, we got up. I went to the kitchen table to think and write. I wanted to put my thoughts about our daughter on paper. My wife's brother and sister-in-law from Montana walked in the kitchen about 4:30 a.m. How had they gotten here so quickly?

They had left immediately and flown their private plane. They knew how we would be feeling. They lost a three-year-old daughter to cancer sixteen years prior to this. They hurt with us; we cried, they tried to comfort us. We talked until early morning, going over what had happened.

DAY 2

Time went by without us noticing. People came and went. We were busy greeting people, exchanging condolences. Later that morning, another of my wife's sisters and her girls came. She had lost two children at birth and knew how we were feeling. Our children seemed to be comforted by her. She knew how we hurt. Time seemed to stand still. We felt no hunger. We were not tired. At the arrival of each relative, our eyes welled up with tears. I thought I couldn't cry anymore, but I was wrong. More tears came and wouldn't stop. Todd (our son) arrived home. He drove all night to get here. His girlfriend came with him. They drove and stopped late and came right away in the morning; the roads were bad. We were glad that someone had come with him. People came and went. More food. More people cared. It was building a bond between the people of our small town and the church and our family. (Why was the damned gun loaded?)

This isn't really happening! It is real! Why do all of these people continue to show up and offer their condolences? It really is true! What did I do that made God mad at me to cause all of this? Why is God taking revenge on me and my family? My daughter's boyfriend walked in the house. All of his brothers and sisters came in with him. We were surprised that he was out of the hospital already. Tears flowed again. The gnawing feeling of what happened was tearing my guts out. I wanted to pray and ask God to help take care of my family, but I couldn't. Not the God that really didn't care about us. We hadn't eaten all day.

I still wasn't hungry. People were now leaving for the night. We were tired, but the night wasn't going to let us sleep. Emotional silence. Lori's boyfriend went home; we hadn't eaten all day. I wanted someone to stay.

DAY 3

We couldn't sleep. I was up early, 4:00 a.m. Reading trying to write—didn't know what to say, kind of like the people that came by—they didn't know what to say either, but at least we were extremely happy that they came by. We all sat at the kitchen table, talked, cried—it was a time of sharing, it was a time of deep hurt—we never ate breakfast. People of the community are fantastic. The owner of the local restaurant brought two dozen homemade rolls. On any other occasion, I would have been tempted to eat three or four without batting an eye. This morning, I was still not hungry. The day started slowly, Debra, Lori's little sister and roommate, didn't want to get out of bed. A good family friend and Debra's BB gun coach happened to stop by. He had lost a brother not too many years before. He spent a lot of time with Debra. I think they talked, cried, and he knew what she was feeling and going through. Thank god for people like Larry.

Lori's boyfriend called and wanted to come over and go for a ride with only me. He wanted to talk. What would I say? The only thing that I could say was what I was feeling. (Why was the damn gun loaded?) I told him that I tried to pray for him but couldn't do it. I told him I was mad and upset because the gun should not have been loaded. I told him we hurt for us. We didn't know how we could go on without our daughter.

DAY 4

Sleep failed to come again that night. We were up early. This is the day of Grandma's farm sale. Everyone had worked hard to prepare for this day. Grandma thought that she should postpone the sale. We said that Lori would not have wanted it that way. Lori wanted to be at this sale. He was a special Grandpa to her. She had come home from college to help take care of him during his illness. He passed away on her birthday a couple of months prior to this date. Now they were selling the farm equipment. I guess she and Grandpa will watch it together. We told her that since he died on her birthday, her next birthday would be special. It always will be.

The doorbell rang. It was early morning. When I opened the door, I was face to face with a complete stranger. He was dressed in a three-piece suit. It was kind of strange in farm country to be calling on someone in a three-piece suit and this early in the morning.

"You don't know who I am. I am your competition in the life insurance industry."

I thought that this was a strange meeting.

"I live in Blunt, South Dakota, a smaller town than where we lived. I sell Lutheran brotherhood insurance. We have never crossed paths in all of these years even though we only live thirty-six miles apart." He went on to say, "I wanted to stop by and tell you how sorry I am for your loss. I wanted to tell you that the people that stop by and tell you that they know how you feel and know what you are going through is completely false. Most of them have never walked in your shoes. They don't have a clue. You see, I do have a clue. My family went through what you are experiencing a few years ago."

I said, "Won't you come in?"

He told me, "No, I know what is going on in there, and I am not going to stay long. You see, my two sons went rabbit hunting in one of our pastures. One of them was leaning out of the window trying to shoot a rabbit, and the other was driving. The one driving hit a hole and rolled the pickup. Rolling it over, killing his younger brother."

"Wow!" I said. "I am so sorry."

He continued, "I wanted to stop and tell you that if you ever need to talk with someone anytime, day or night, I am available and I do know what you are going through and how you feel."

With that, he gave me his business card and walked away. It was really strange, but today, I know exactly how he felt.

LORINDA

I cry, I weep, I hurt. How does anyone cope with this pain? This emptiness? It hurts so bad, so deep—will it ever be okay? Lori was bouncy, she was vibrant, she was truly a beautiful person. She wrote little notes to her friends. She wrote letters to them and never gave what she wrote to them. She had deep emotions. She hurt for everyone. She got hurt easily. She loved life. "Don't quit" became her motto. I gave her a poem one time when she was hurt. "Don't quit," she wrote it on a piece of paper as a thought for the day (September 21, 1988).

> When things go wrong as they sometimes will
> When the road you're trudging seems all uphill
> When the funds are low and the debts are high
> When you want to smile; but have to sigh
> When care is pressing you down a bit-
> Rest if you must--but don't you quit!!
> Life is queer with its twists and turns,
> As everyone of us sometimes learns,
> And many a person has turned about
> When they might have won if they stuck it out.
> Don't give up though the pace seems slow
> You may succeed with just another blow.
> Often the struggler has given up
> When they might have captured the victor's cup

And learned too late when the night came down
How close he was to the golden gate.
Success is failure turned inside out.
The silver tint of the clouds of doubt.
So, stick to the fight when you are hardest hit,
It is when things go wrong that you mustn't quit

Author Unknown

Her thought of the day was the verse I had given her to hang on wall to read daily. She didn't need to copy it down but wanted a friend to have it.

Funeral Arrangements

It hurts; the pain seems to be agonizing. How does my wife stand it? She doesn't. She hurts, she cries, she screams at the emptiness. How are my children living with the emptiness? The nothingness? The loneliness? This is forever; there is no turning back.

We had to make plans for the family service and funeral. Was this for her? Was this for us? We sat in the early morning at the kitchen table. What are we supposed to do? How are we really supposed to feel? We started to write down on paper thoughts about our daughter. I laughed at memories, I cried, I hurt. She had been a real part of our life. She would burst into the room, smiling, "What do you think, Dad?" Hitting me on the arm. She was my baby. How could we go on?

What could we say at the funeral? We wanted everyone to know our daughter. She liked everything to be just right. When Grandpa died, she wanted to pick out the clothes he would wear. She wanted him to wear his new boots. She wanted him to have a little money to take with him. She knew he needed a little money to buy coffee. She wanted him to have a family picture next to his heart.

We had to go to the flower shop and funeral home. We wanted our family to have a say in these decisions. The rest of the family had some real definite ideas on what Lori would have liked. We picked a casket wreath of red roses, a lot of roses—Lori loved roses. We put her Snow Queen crown in the middle of the roses. It would have been what Lori would have done.

At the funeral home, the director sat with all of us for a while. He said this was the hardest funeral he had ever done. He cried softly, not trying to show his emotions. He told us how we would be looking at caskets and vaults and how to determine the prices. He took us to the showroom with the different models. Then he left so we could make up our minds. It was hard. I knew my daughter was in the next room. He wouldn't let us see her now, but I knew she was there and it hurt to the core.

My children decided on a light blue casket with a plush blue interior. Again, Lori would have liked their choice.

When we arrived at the house, the minister was there to plan the family service and funeral. Our minister was hurting also. He had told me on several occasions that he didn't know if he could do the service. He didn't know if he could talk about Lori without being emotional. I told him with God's help, he would be able to do just fine. I didn't believe what I was telling him. I didn't believe this God would help anyone. He had stolen my daughter from me. Why would he be here to help the minister?

We picked out favorite songs, favorite scripture. We asked Lori's boyfriend's family to do some readings and sing. They wanted to. We planned the family service for the night before the funeral.

What an agonizing decision—should we allow people to see her body? Should we allow the children to see her? We decided to open the casket for viewing for a short while on Sunday afternoon.

FAMILY SERVICE

It was surprisingly peaceful to see her there. I knew she really wasn't there. It was just the shell of the body that housed her spirit while she was in the world. I didn't want to leave her. It hurt with a hurt that is indescribable.

We went back for the family service. It was tough walking into that church. Flowers from everywhere adorned the church building. The funeral director told us more flowers would be coming on the late bus. I had never seen so many flowers at a funeral. They were enormously appreciated, but I didn't want flowers replacing my little girl. I didn't think I could stand the hurt. I wanted to run and scream. I wanted to leave. What were my kids thinking? They had to be hurting as badly as I was. How could I be so selfish to not notice their feelings, their emotions, their hurting? I have to be strong for them, for my wife. I had forgotten about visiting with each child the past few days. The school system had let students come over at various times to be with the children. It was good. They went to their bedrooms and shared with the other kids. The guidance counselor showed up on several occasions. She was a really big help. I had been involved with my own feelings; I didn't consider theirs.

Lori would have liked the family service. Friends told how she was—it was Lori! She was blunt with them, always finding ways to get them together. Forever doing little things for them. Promoting birthday parties, special occasion parties, and just plain parties. She would make them birthday cakes; cherry cheesecake was her favorite, microwave popcorn was her specialty. I hate using the word "was." I will always have Lori with me. She is everywhere I look. She is at the beginning of every sentence. She is at the ending of every paragraph. She will always be a part of me.

DAY 5

Sleep wouldn't come again tonight. How could she be gone? (Why was that gun loaded?) Laughter around the dinner table would never be the same. I loved to tease her. I loved to torment her. I loved her.

How deep can a person have pain? My family has a wound that tears out their hearts. I want to reach out and heal it for them. I can't. I can't reach that far. I can't reach that deep. I want my wound healed. I want my family to be whole again. I want my son to be able to be best friends with his baby sister. I want her to be alive.

Everyone that comes to the house hurts. They don't have any idea of what to say. Some people tell us it was the Lord's will. I don't believe them. I really don't want to listen to them. I listen. I talk. It does make me feel better for the moment. Every time I glance at my wife, I see terrible pain in her eyes. We love each other. We love the children. It could have been worse. I could have had to face all of this by myself. I love my wife. I love my children.

Letters, cards, flowers from everywhere pour in. Letters and cards from people we don't even know. They are sharing their tragedies, their losses. It still hurts, but it is comforting knowing that with time, the wound will scab over but not completely heal.

This was the day I dreaded! February 27, 1989. This is the day we were to cover her body with dirt. I wanted her to be comfortable. I took three stuffed animals that she had, her favorite we had gotten her for Christmas. A blue cuddly thing—I'm not sure what you called it, but she would hold it when she was upset. She would hold it and pout. I loved her pout. We had asked the funeral director if we could spend some time with her that morning and say goodbye. I stood there by her side. I had a flashback of when she was small. I had picked her up when she was only a few hours old, had held her with my rough hands. She was soft, gentle. She was always soft and gentle. I always held her. I rocked her to sleep, and of course, at times, I had to use these same hands to reprimand her. Now, she lay there still and silent. I reached down and touched her; she was cold and almost like porcelain. I needed to touch her, I needed to see her; it was my way of saying goodbye but not forever. I picked a beautiful rose and placed it in her hand. I wanted her to take with her the flower she loved. I also placed a picture of our family close to her heart. The children had picked out her clothes and the necklace that her boyfriend had given her. He also wanted to her to have his class ring, which was on the same chain as her necklace. We all loved her. We will miss her beyond words.

I didn't want to go to the funeral—a thousand people showed up. She had touched the hearts from several states. People don't understand why I'm crying. While I'm writing this, I cry for my loss, not for God's gain.

I do believe in God, but I don't like what he did to my family. We are supposed to be tested, but this is a tough test to take.

The songs were sung with deep emotion, beautiful words, and beautiful voices. Lori would have been proud. Everyone that gave a testimony never faltered, never stuttered, did it with deep conviction and emotion. It was a tremendous service. The minister, with God's help, gave a heartwarming service. I was numb. I was having to go through this. I tried to daydream about the good times, remembering the poem I had found in my office drawer the day before she died. She had written a poem in the first grade about her bike. She even drew a picture and had some misspelled words as always.

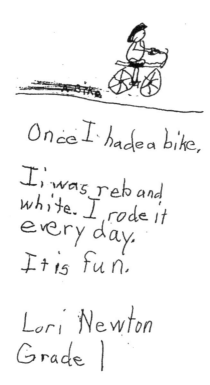

Once I had a bike,
I was reb and
white. I rode it
every day.
It is fun.

Lori Newton
Grade 1

We laughed when I showed it to her. She wanted it for her memories. My thoughts turned to what I had found in her Bible that very morning. I smiled to myself. Lori had written a letter to a friend of hers by the name of Galen. She had written the letter four years ago, urging him to become baptized. She wanted to make sure he would be in heaven with her someday. The letter read:

Dear Galen

Tonight, as I was reading my Bible, I was thinking of you and thinking that you haven't made your choice to be baptized yet. So I looked up baptism and found some verses that might help you in your decision. I know it is a hard thing to do 'cause when I decided to get baptized, I really didn't know who to tell or how to go about it, and I was really scared of it. Because I thought that being baptized meant that you had to follow the "rules"—no bad stuff, ya know—but Dad explained to me that God will forgive you of your sins after you are baptized just the same as he did before. Just that now he knows that you have officially turned your life over to him. It's kinda just like the first step to a long-lasting project. A project that decides eternity! I guess what I'm trying to tell you is that it is a good chance to take because if you take it, you will be on the path to a sure win, and if you don't, Galen, I'm afraid of the ending. I don't know how much you've thought about it or even if you have already made your decision, but I just wanted you to know that I'm thinking about and praying for you! I really hope some of these verses help 'cause I want to see you in heaven, OK! You know if you ever need someone to help you make this decision and don't know who to go to, don't be afraid to talk to me about it, OK. If you don't feel comfortable talking to me, talk to my Dad 'cause you know he is behind you 100 percent and that he loves you guys lots.

Well, I guess this is a good-enough lecture 'cause I have to go to bed, so I'll be able to get up for church tomorrow.

P.S. I ask only one more thing!
If you are not ready, don't let me or anyone else pressure you into it. You have to do what's best for you and God. OK!

Love ya lots,
Lorinda

P.S. Thanks for reading this. I hope it made a little bit of sense anyway.

Then Jesus came from Galilee to the Jordan to be baptized by John. But John tried to deter him, saying, "I need to be baptized by you, and do you come to me?" Jesus replied, "Let it be so now; it is proper for us to do this to fulfill all righteousness." As soon as Jesus was Baptized, he went out of the water. At that moment heaven was opened and he saw the Spirit of God descending like a dove and lighting on him. And a voice from heaven said, "This is my Son, whom I love; with him I am well pleased." (Matthew 3:13–7)

Now Jesus himself was about 30 years old when he began his ministry. (& when he was Baptized). (Luke 3:23)

And this water symbolizes baptism that now saves you also—not the removal of dirt from the body but the pledge of a good conscience toward God. It saves you by the resurrection of Jesus Christ who has gone to heaven & is at God's right hand—with angels, authorities & powers in submission to him. (1 Peter 3:21)

Also, you can read Colossians 2:11–3:11, Hebrew 6:2, and Ephesians 4:5.

We shared the letter at the funeral. We wanted everyone to know what our daughter was really like. Some that came to the funeral had not even met her, but now they could know that she was concerned for everyone, even them.

To Lori

I smiled again as I recalled a short note I had also found in her Bible. It must have been written when she was a freshman in high school. It read:

Dear Mommy and Daddy,

Thank you for grounding me. It will help me to grow—I think!

This was definitely our girl—she always had hesitations. We loved her for that. We showed our feelings about her. We had my sister read the following at the funeral.

Lori had a rebellious personality from the time she was born.

At one week, she started waking in the middle of the night. Wide awake, we would say, "Lori, it's night, you have to go back to sleep," but she wouldn't.

At seven months, we said, "Lori, you mustn't pull Todd's hair," but she did.

At two, we said, "Lori, you have to help pick up your toys," she wouldn't.

At four, we said, "Lori, you have to eat your peas," she didn't.

At six, we said, "Lori, please clean up your room," and she would show us with pride her tidy room, only to find out everything was stuffed under her bed.

While playing cards at ten, we said, "You can't look at the other kid's hands," but she did.

In junior high, we said, "You shouldn't get those kind of movies to watch with your friends," but she did.

At fifteen, we said, "Lori, you have to follow the rules," but she didn't.

At sixteen, we said, "You can't wear your sister's clothes without their permission," but she did.

At eighteen, we said, "Don't lay in the sun, don't eat other people's candy," but she did.

At nineteen, we said, "Eat nutritious food, buckle your seatbelt, and don't drive so fast, and please be quiet when you come in late," but she wouldn't.

There was another side of Lori.

At birth, she was a beautiful baby.

At seven months, she gave her brother kisses.

At two, she was his constant companion.

At ten, she loved her beautiful black cat named Cinder.

In junior high, her friends came first in her life.

At sixteen, she was full of vim, vigor, and vitality. Ready to take on the world, baking cherry cheesecakes for her classmate's birthdays, she was busy loving the world. This year, she gave her life to Christ.

At eighteen, she was a busy student body vice president, making sure everyone kept the school spirit and had a good time.

At nineteen, she was busy making micro-wave popcorn, working for her parents or at the nursing home, indulging in her favorite pastime of being a sister, loving her classmates and family, and being the greatest daughter in the world.

Lori, we will always love you.

Her parents,
Mike and DJ

The cemetery was cold. The wind was blowing hard, but I didn't notice the cold. My wife was shaking but probably not from the cold. She was more concerned that other people were going to get cold. I remember the minister, starting the Lord's Prayer. I didn't want this to be final, but it was final—really final!

The kids picked roses from the casket spray and put them in the vault with her. I hadn't told them I had given her one to hold. She would take them with her.

Friends and relatives showed up from several states—about four hundred stayed for lunch after the funeral. We were still not hungry. Food looked terrible. We tried to greet and thank as many people as we could for coming. We couldn't get to everyone.

Later that afternoon, everyone was leaving to go home; even though we had the rest of our family, loneliness was really starting to set in. Where was Lori? Why wasn't she coming home? Why wasn't she walking in the door? The hurt was still there. We spent a quiet evening at home. Our son called; he had gotten back to college. (Thank God). We are nervous about all our children leaving the house.

LATER

The next few days passed slowly. We tried to go to work. I would sit at my desk and not seem to know what was going on. People would come in, and I would think, *Don't you know that we covered our little girl with dirt? How can you forget about it and be normal and happy?*

A mist which soft breeze drives off,
A flutter of finch through bushes,
A fall of snow,
Candle's flickering flame,
Lily of a day's endurance,
So fleeting is our existence,
A slip of the foot,
Swerve
Gasp
Growth inside
A shot
And we are gone.

> *"I heard a voice say 'cry'. I said, 'What shall I cry?'*
> *'Cry this,' said the voice: All flesh is grass, and all its*
> *beauty is like the flower of the field. The grass with-*
> *ers, the flower fades, when the breath of the Lord*
> *blows upon it; surely the people is grass." (Isaiah 40)*

RUSTY

I found another writing of my daughter. Two years ago, one of her grandfather's horses became terribly sick. I had to put the horse out of its misery. She wrote a letter to her favorite horse called Rusty:

Once upon a time when I was a little girl, the world never seemed to change. That only seems like yesterday. But now, my world has started to crumble away, and my yesterdays are almost a faint memory passed off in the moonlight. This place is hell for some, but for me, all things around it and all things in it were a paradise, but those dreams are now slipping away for time changes all.

I suppose that is the way it is supposed to be—that things change. Because if things always stayed the same, I would not be as strong as I am today. Things that happen in life are hard to accept sometimes, but I guess we will just have to take them as they come and use them as stepping-stones to make ourselves stronger day by day.

And this is no exception.

I will always cherish my precious memory of my big friend who was always there for me, but I failed to be there for her and that hurts.

I'll miss you, Rusty.

Now, I put this away under lock and key 'cause Grandpa says that's the way it's supposed to be.

I don't know if I can just put it to past.

How can I?

Rusty was too sweet and kind
She brought out my good side
And yes, sometimes my bad, but
She was always my friend.
When we were together
I hadn't a care
So how do they dare make me pack her memory away in my heart somewhere?
But Grandpa is older and wiser, and his will must be done
So I guess time continues changing, just as the setting sun.

THE WORLD IS SMALLER

The world is different now. Things that seemed to be a mountain yesterday are nothing more than a pebble today. The petty grievances that were big problems are dismissed as trifle matters. People shouldn't have problems with their children. Parents should feel ecstasy for having their children still with them. The mountains don't seem to be as attractive; the river doesn't seem to have as much magic. Will the appeal of the mountains and the magic of the river ever come back? How will I answer questions when people ask: will all of your children be home for Christmas or Easter? What will I say? Will I say yes or will I explain and say no?

"What are all of your kids doing for summer work? Will I count all six or just say what the five will be doing? How many children do you have?"

Will I tell them about Lori or just let it pass?

Innocent questions I know will hurt. They already hurt before they are asked.

It's been three weeks since Lori's tragic accident. We still start each day and end each day with tears. There are plenty of times during the day that little reminders trigger a swell of tears. It seems to be a little easier to talk with people, but the wound is still awfully deep.

God is still not a particular favorite being in my life. I still have many unanswered questions. My wife and I are searching the Bible and other commentaries to find answers to our questions. I'm not sure there are answers, just questions. Friends I have that are non-Christian will tell me that there is no God. If there were a God, he wouldn't do things like this. The God of the Bible is not supposed to hurt people, only love them. The minister is trying to help. He is trying to understand.

Friends are still calling wanting to help, to talk. They're great! The people at church have already forgotten how small and unimportant some matters are compared to life itself. They are already starting to bicker over trivial things. How easily people forget.

My little daughter continually writes the names of each person in our family, including Lori's, with a postscript saying, "Good family." She writes these names on a chalkboard and on paper. She also draws hearts with Lori's name on the inside saying Lori loves everybody. Here is a picture of one of those hearts:

Each member of the family hurts. They have to have their own grief. I've determined that grief and sorrow are OK unless you carry it too long and too far. As of yet, I don't know how long is too long and how far is too far. On Sunday evening, just one and a half weeks after Lori had died, I was sitting at the kitchen table trying to type. I thought if I typed what I was writing, it would be faster. Not me, I don't type very well. I decided to put the typewriter back in Lori's closet. When I left her room, I noticed a drawer in her dresser was left open, so I went to close it. I noticed some pictures in the front of the drawer and picked them up to look at it. They were pictures of Lori and some of her friends. I noticed a small envelope, which had no address on it, so I opened it to find what was in it. When I read it, I wept. I hurt. I was confused. I was alone in the house. I sat for a long time pondering the contents of that envelope. It was a handwritten will that Lori had done at some time prior to her death. It read:

> Mom and Dad
> Todd, Brenda, Debra, Monica, and Sarah
>
> This isn't really what it seems like. Don't even think of me as being gone because I'm not. I will always be here in your minds and in your hearts. And you can always talk to me because I will be listening. Brenda, I want you to have my car because you will need it when you go away for school. Tell Dad to use some of my life insurance money to pay it off for you. Debra, you will miss sleeping with me. I know! Ha! Ha! But knowing how much you love my clothes, they are all yours. But as far as the room goes, Debra, you can leave it the way it is. What's mine is now yours. I would like it very much though if you would please give Treg my Puff-a-lump. Sarah and Monica, you two little birds mean a lot to me, and there is nothing I wouldn't do for you—I just wanted you to know that. I want you

two to share my ghetto blaster, OK? Whatever Debra doesn't want in the room that is mine, you can have first chance at. Todd, you being a boy and all, well, I don't suppose you want my clothes or makeup, so I want you to have my big red bear you gave me for Xmas. I love that bear, so take good care of it. I would like Treg to have my luggage, all of it! (For graduation) Mom and Dad, I love you both very much! Thank you for standing by me when I wasn't such an angel, but I do think you did a good job of raising me 'cause I think I turned out OK. Mom, Brenda will have to take my beautician spot! When you go to Ireland, I don't want you to worry about the kids because they will be fine. Brenda and Debra, do a good job! Take care of yourselves. I love you all! And remember, don't worry, be happy. Right, Dad!

I Love You
Lorinda Lynn Newton

P.S. Sarah and Monica, would you please take care of Cinder for me! She needs to be fed—and give her lots of love and attention.

I let my wife see it that evening. She had the same reaction: we were devastated. Did Lori know something we had not known? What was the meaning of this letter? How could she write this with the touch of humor that depicted my girl? We will cling to the letter and eventually show it to the rest of the children.

Sunday came; it was time to go to church. I hate going in that church building. All I see when I enter the church building is a casket in front where the communion table is and flowers adorning the entire front of the stage. I think it will take years for this feeling to pass. I have to make peace with myself. Man, that is hard to do. This morning, it was especially hard for me to be there. I was supposed to give the communion meditation. I wasn't prepared. I didn't know what to say. I didn't know if I could stand up there and talk about God. I didn't feel close to God. It was tough. I sat in church. I could not sing. I couldn't do anything but stare. Stare at the front, at the mirage. The casket I saw that wasn't there, at the flowers I couldn't see or smell. What would I say? Would I be able to give the meditation?

During one of the songs, I opened my Bible. It fell open to a passage in Luke. I looked down. I had marked in yellow a passage about the death of Jesus.

> *"It was now about the sixth hour and darkness came over the whole land until the ninth hour. For the sun stopped shining and the curtain of the temple was torn in two."*

The sun had stopped shining in our life. The curtain of the temple was torn in two. I looked at these words for several minutes. I stared. I was blank. Our sun definitely had stopped shining. Would it ever shine again? Our temple was divided; would it ever be united? I thought God must have suffered a real sorrow, a real grief that he had to have his son suffer the way he did so that we who believe might have that everlasting life. Lori believed. I thought maybe I should share this verse. I read on:

> *"Jesus called out with a loud voice. Father into your hands I commit my spirit. When he had said this, he had breathed his last." (1)*

Lori had breathed her last. She didn't have time to tell the Lord that into His hands she committed her spirit, but three years prior to her death, she already had given her life to the Lord. She definitely lived a Christian life. She also shared her testimony with the world. She depicted a life people could follow. She tried to lead people to her Jesus.

> *"The centurion had seen what happened, praised God and said, 'Surely this was a righteous man.' When all the people that had gathered to watch, this sight saw what took place, beat their breast and*

walked away. But all those that knew him including the women that followed him from Galilee stood at a distance and watched these things." (2)

Lori was a righteous person. People had gathered to watch. People had gathered for the family service. People had gathered for the funeral. After these things were over, the crowd dispersed. People went home. We went home without Lori!

Our friends and relatives are tremendous people. They are still there when we need them the most. These are the people that make up our world. We love them for being just friends.

1) Matthew 22:45–46
2) Matthew 22:50

LORI NEWTON
December 3, 1969 - February 22, 1989

 Funeral services were held Monday, February 27, for Lorinda Lynn Newton, who died February 22, 1989, two miles south of Highmore. Pastor Merlin Bartel officiated and burial was in Highmore City Cemetery.

Pallbearers were Brad Hall, Jason Pekarek, Shaun Baloun, Bruce Bucholz, Darin Larson, and James Kindopp. Honorary casket bearers were the members of Highmore High School Class of 1988.

Lorinda Lynn Newton was born December 3, 1969, at Gregory, South Dakota, to Michael and Donna Jean (Hamlin) Newton. She was baptized at the Church of Christ, Highmore, South Dakota. She lived with her family in several towns during her early life, coming to Highmore when she was ten years old. Her vibrant, caring, loving youth brought her many friends and encouraged her in her many activities.

While in High School, she was involved in girls' basketball as a student manager and also an avid Pirate fan at all other sports activities. She was also active in drama, FHA, FBLA, debate, Hisodak and many other activities. She served as vice president of the Student Council and was an Honor Student.

She had the honor of being crowned Miss Highmore at the 1987 Snow Queen Pageant. She was an active member of the Church of Christ.

She was employed part-time at the Highmore Nursing Home and was presently enrolled as a student at Capital University in Pierre, South Dakota, studying to become a surgical technician.

Survivors include: her parents of Highmore, one brother, Michael Todd, Fargo, N. Dakota; four sisters: Brenda, Debra, Monica and Sarah, all of Highmore; paternal grandparents, Mr. & Mrs. E.L. Newton; maternal grandmother, Mrs. Gordon Hamlin, Highmore; and a host of aunts, uncles and cousins, She was preceded in death by her grandfather, Gordon Hamlin, and three cousins.

First Sunday at Church: Communion

I walked to the front of the church, past the casket that wasn't there, past the flowers I couldn't see or smell. I walked to the lectern. Opening my Bible to the verse in Luke, I stood there without words. I began to talk. I told the people this was hard to do. I related the correlation between our tragedy and the suffering and tragedy of Jesus hanging on the tree—stripped of his clothes, stripped of his humanity, his pride, hanging there with only his love for the father and the people that believe in him. I told them we could lose our earthly bodies and our losses could be considered great, but there is no reason why we would have to lose the love of Christ. We would not have to lose Christ out of our world, of our lives.

The sun didn't shine in our life. I know God didn't want us to be sorrowful over the death of a Christian. But that is impossible, especially when that loss is so close and so great. This did give me a certain amount of comfort. When I sat down, tears were flowing freely down my cheeks. I did stand up in front of the congregation. I did give the meditation. I wasn't sure what I was going to say when I got up there, and I'm not sure what I really said after I sat down.

That morning, the minister preached out of the book of Job. This was probably his tenth sermon from Job. I knew Lori liked this book of the Bible. Job should not have had to go through all the problems that he faced. God, how could any human being go through this many problems and still come to grips with the God that brought him to his knees'? I guess maybe that might be what God wants us to do is be brought to our knees. I listened intently to what the minister was saying. My thoughts started to wander to the people that wrote us letters. Thinking about the tragedies and losses other people had in their lives. Thinking about the multiple tragedies in their lives. We received a letter from a lady several states away. She started the letter:

"I don't know you people and you don't know me, but I do want to tell you that the only way you are going to be able to make it through is to make peace with yourself and with God. I think I can safely speak on this and would encourage you to consider this. I lost a seventeen-month-old son that drowned in a church baptistery while my husband and I were working in church. A few years later, I lost my husband in a work-related fire, and just a few shorts years ago, I lost a seventeen-year-old son in an accident with a shotgun."

How could this woman stand to be alive? Human beings have had more losses than our family, but that doesn't lessen the grief or the loss. Our tragedy is great, our loss is great, but maybe only we know how great and how deep it hurts. We can't share that with the world. It has to be personal. Maybe someday when the wound scabs over and the scar is left, I'll be able to feel what others that have devastating tragedies are going through. Maybe I'll be able to be a small help. Maybe I can walk in their shoes for a while. Maybe I can have empathy. Maybe I will be able to help. Maybe this is what God wanted? Maybe? Maybe? Maybe? There are a lot of questions. These questions are just questions and, probably in my earthly life, will none of them be answered.

It has been a month to the day that Lori went away. It seems like yesterday. She is still on every thought. I need to talk about her. I need to write about her. I'm still waiting for her to bounce into the room.

At times, I am overwhelmed by the trouble in my world.

I shut my eyes to make it go away. It doesn't. When I open my eyes, I see Lori everywhere. I'm amazed at what people think of as real problems. They don't have problems, just detours in life. When I am hurt, I have the desire to say, "But I was good. Why did this happen to my world?" I have to "grow up" to the knowledge that God never promised a life free from trouble; his son said, "I have said this to you, that in me you may find peace. In the world, you have tribulation; but be of good cheer, I have overcome the world."

Lori has overcome the world, but I haven't yet accepted her absence. I doubt if I'll ever be able to.

Six Years Later

The storm clouds have lifted somewhat over the past six years. There is not a day goes by that I still have a small tear or an emotional moment when I stop and think of my daughter. It has become much easier to talk about her with the children. I am now convinced that even though I was angry with God in the beginning, his sustaining love and my deep faith has brought me safely to this point. It seems clear to me that people who worship God in the good times can have someone to turn to during the cloudy times. If you have that deep faith during the good times, then God will give you the inner strength during the moments of crisis. He will become much closer to your life than ever before.

I would like to end with a poem someone gave me. The author is unknown.

A Sparrow Fell

A sparrow fell—and no one heard.
Nobody cared. It was just a bird.
From all the numberless flitting throng
Of sparrows, who would miss one song?
But God leaned down and whispered, "I care.
It was one of MY sparrows, and I WAS THERE
A little girl, all sunshine and laughter,
(And sometimes scolding's, with kisses after!)
And hurts to smooth over, and deeds to applaud
A little girl fell! Where were you, God?
A little girl fell! God, why weren't you there?
Is it only for sparrows and such that You care?
If you're God at all—then you could have prevented
This nightmare of pain! So You must have consented,
I've always believed You were loving and good.
I'd like to believe still—if only I could.
But God if You Love me, how can You allow
Such unbearable pain as I'm feeling right now?
Such helplessness—hopelessness—bitter regret—
So many tears that have fallen; and yet
So many more that are still locked inside.
Oh, God—out there somewhere—have you ever cried?
I'm not even sure, anymore, that You're real.
But if You are, God—Do you care how I feel?

****

Beloved, I care! In the midst of your grief,
In the midst of your stricken and crumbling disbelief,
In the midst of the blackness of total despair,
In the midst of your questioning, Child—I am there.
In the midst! Not far off in some vague fifth dimension,
But there, where you are,
Giving you My attention
My constant attention—and not just today.
Since before you were born, I have loved you this way.
You're important to Me. Every hair on your head
I have numbered Myself! Can these tears that you shed
Go uncounted? Unnoticed? Nay, child; here I stand
Close enough that each tear drop falls into My hand.

This was the last song sung at my daughter's funeral. I still have tears in my eyes 10,220 days later whenever I listen to this song.

A close friend of my daughter's had an extra groomsman at her wedding. He wasn't walking with anyone. This was written on the back of her wedding booklet. (We cried when we saw this.)

In Loving Memory

Lorinda Lynn Newton born December 3, 1969. and died in a tragic accident February 22, 1989.

Lori, I leave this place open in your honor, Your friendship and love are unreplaceable. I asked you to stand with me and share this special day with me just as we always shared everything, the good things, the bad things, the fun things, and the sad things. And today, in my heart you are here sharing with me. You will forever be in my heart.

I love you always, Lori,

Several Years Later

In the pursuit of joy and happiness, I was asked to give the sermon at church one Sunday. I had no idea what to speak about, but the Lord told me to speak on a journey of joy and happiness. (I wasn't sure I could do this.)

This is the sermon as I remember.

On this day, every year little boys across the Americas and around the world dream big dreams. They may not say so, but inside their heads are mental images of themselves being viewed by millions of people all around the world. In their imaginations, they will one day wear the uniform and be a part of some championship team battling for the ultimate trophy, a sparkling silver trophy in the shape of a football and a Super Bowl ring that will fit on their size 18 finger. We call this Sunday Super Bowl Sunday. Amazingly, a few of those little boys who dream big dreams do wind up playing in the big game. Over thirty years ago when the first Super Bowl was played, a ten-year-old boy sat beside his father in the stands of the Los Angeles Coliseum. He watched players like Bart Starr, Paul Hornung, Boyd Dowler, Fuzy Thusrston, Carrol Dale, and other outstanding athletes on Vince Lombardi's great Green Bay Packers football team. He watched as Green Bay dominate their opponents. He daydreamed of one day being on the gridiron. That is exactly what happened. James Lofton, a wide receiver for the Buffalo Bills, finally made it to the top and had his dream come true. Through strong and weak seasons, team changes, and several injuries as a football player, Loften persevered; his determination paid off. The Bills haven't won a Super Bowl in three tries, but James Lofton played in two of them.

I can't tell you what makes football fans out of people, but I can tell you why I follow the game with such interest far beyond the brutality of the smashing and pounding, the aches and pains of the game, I see an analogy between football and life. Those who hang tough, refusing to give up no matter how difficult or demanding or disappointing the challenges may be, are the ones that stand the best chance of winning. They are the ones that find some of the greatest satisfaction and happiness on earth.

Joy and happiness comes to those who are determined to pursue it despite the circumstances. As the poet says:

> One ship sails east
> One ship sails west
> Regardless of how the wind blows
> It is the set of the sail
> And not the gale
> That determines the way you go.
>
> (author unknown)

Happiness and joy have nothing to do with one's age, occupation, geography, education, marital status, goods, looks, or circumstances. Happiness and joy comes from confidence in God. If we have God involved in our lives and what we are doing, what we are about to do, and all of our plans, how can we not find joy and happiness? Happiness and joy have nothing to do with anything external regardless of how rough the winds of adversity blow or how big the waves are we cross, we need to set our sails in the direction of God and he will take us to joy and happiness. Listen to what Paul says in Philippians 1:12–14:

> *"Now I want you to know brothers, that what has happened to me has really served to advance the gospel as a result, it has become clear throughout the whole Palace guard and to everyone else that I'm in*

chains for Christ (but) because of my chains, most of the brothers in the lord have been encouraged to speak the word of God more courageously and fearlessly."

It is deplorable how negative thinking can get you down. Paul didn't allow his feelings and attitude and his place of domicile while he was in prison to get him down. Gloom and doom seem to be our attitudes today. We seem to have a free spirit when we are born and we probably even have it with a smile, as we cried our way into this world. Then we seem to start losing our spirit of happiness and joy when we reach about the third and fourth grades in school. Kids already in the fifth grade start worrying about who likes who, and if he is buddies with him, then I can't be buddies with that guy. Maybe something was said at home about the kid's parents, then the grade schoolers take it to school and others don't want to be friends with those parents' kids. Then junior high switches to which girl likes which boy and vice versa. Sometimes, for some people, this never stops. Then we make it to high school, then college, then into the real world, and we end up with more of the same that we experienced in our formative years. Hopefully, we make it to retirement then what? Do we ever stop worrying? Most of us have forgotten to put God into all of our plans along the way (there goes happiness and joy) and we wonder why.

When you substitute worry for living with God, then you have to be the one to take the responsibility for your problems. As we saw in Paul's circumstances, he gave the worrying to God. We still have to deal with the circumstances of life, but if we put it in God's hands, we can deal with.

It's easier once we accept him as our Lord and Savior.

Do not commit spiritual suicide. Let me tell you a story about a man that lived life to the fullest; he thought that he and his family were good Christians. He and his wife spent time taking them to church and Sunday school and taught Sunday school to make sure the kids learned of God. They prayed before every meal and made sure they were at meals with everyone. He was extremely proud of his wife and children and the way they were growing in the Lord.

They dreamed of the days when money problems would be less and the kids would all graduate from school and get good jobs and have their own families. Then one night, he received word of a tragedy that shook his entire world. One of his children had been killed. Stunned with shock and pale with grief, his world had crumbled in an instant. He stumbled through the next week, the next month, and the next years. He realized there was a void that couldn't be filled. He wouldn't know any grandkids, wouldn't walk her down the aisle to get married. The world seemed over for him. Life became meaningless, lost sleep, couldn't eat, started drinking, and became bitter with God. He lost all joy and happiness. He lost all faith in life and with God. He had not set his sails in any direction. He was being blown freely and all directions where the wind blew. A friend finally cracked a two by four over his head, told him that life deals us some terrible hands, but life has to go on. Even though he would never be able to see any grandkids or take them waterskiing or fishing or take them on vacations and read them bedtime stories, he needed to make peace with his God, his wife, and his family. He began to see friends again, began to share with his wife and children. He set his sails on joy and happiness and the direction of Jesus Christ. In 1991, I was able to renounce spiritual suicide. I was able to live once again and put my full commitment in the Lord Jesus Christ because the father of that beautiful nineteen-year-old girl who was killed was myself. You have to put God into everything that you do and have to have confidence to live life to the fullest. This will allow you to laugh more at life; it will allow you to outdistance any uncertainties of life that will surely be thrown your way.

I want you to take a walk with me to the university hospital in Minneapolis, Minnesota. Everyone here has at some time either been in a hospital room as a patient or visitor. Picture with me this scene. Two elderly gentlemen both seriously sick, one lying in a bed next to a window and the other in a bed on the side of the room. The man next to the window is allowed to sit up only for an hour each day to drain the fluid from his lungs. The one not next to the window has to lay flat on his back and can't sit up. The two men talked for hours about their lives, their families, their jobs, their time in the military, their vacations, and anything else they could think about. Every afternoon, when the man next to the only window in the room sat up, he would tell the other what he saw out of the window. The other man started to live just for that hour when he could hear what was outside. When he would broaden his views of the outside world by describing in beautiful detail of what was on the outside. He told him that the window overlooked a park with an expanding lake and bushes and flowers that were all the colors of the rainbow. Ducks and swans played in the water and were not bothered by all of the children playing on some swings and walking their dogs. He would explain in detail the model boats that the children and their parents were motoring around the lake. He even described the type of fish some of the children were able to catch from the lake. Lovers walked arm in arm amid the beautiful flowers and the grand oak trees that graced the shores and the landscape with the view of the city in the background. As the man described the view, the other man would close his eyes and picture the fantastic view in his imagination.

One afternoon, the man at the window described in detail a parade that was passing by. The man lying down could see every detail in his mind. Then, a horrible thought crossed into his mind. He became terribly jealous of the man next to the window. *Why should he be able to see all of that and I am not next to the window?*

As the thought first occurred, he felt ashamed, but as the man described the scenes on a daily basis, the man grew more and more resentful of his situation, and finally, envy soon turned into rage, and the rage turned to anger. He began to pout and found himself not able to sleep. He should be the one by the window. He should have to able to see that view himself; he could push himself up and watch all of that scenery himself. Late one night, he was lying there, staring at the ceiling when the man next to the window began to cough and choke. He was choking on the fluid from his lungs. Listening from across the room, he could hear the man struggling to try to reach for the button to call the nurse. He knew he was groping for the button but was coughing so bad, he couldn't reach it. The man kept coughing and choking and struggling, while the man on his back pretended to be asleep. Soon the choking and coughing stopped, and there was nothing but silence. Deathly silence.

The following morning, the day nurse arrived to take care of her duties for the morning. She found the lifeless body of the man next to the window. No words, no-fuss attendants removed the body, and when the appropriate time had passed, the man asked if it would be all right if he could be moved over by the window? The nurse was more than happy to oblige him. She moved him and made him comfortable before she left the room. Slowly, painfully, he propped himself up on one elbow to take his first look out of the window so he could see the lake and the people. Finally, he would have the joy of seeing it all for himself. He strained to look out of the window beside his bed. His eyes opened wide with amazement. He was staring at a brick wall.

Paul's words to the church at Corinth: "By all this be encouraged. In addition to our own encouragement, we were especially delighted to see how happy Titus was, because his spirit has been refreshed by all of you."

The man by the window was trying to refresh the other's spirit. We should do that for others and allow others to do this for us without the emotions of jealousy and envy you see/the man beside the window was totally blind.

Remember, whoever sows sparingly reaps sparingly and whoever sows generously will reap generously Jesus told us in Luke 6:38: "Give, and it will be given to you. A good measure, pressed down. Shaken, together and running over, will be poured into your lap. For with the measure you give, it will be measured onto you."

Use your smile and give it away every single day. It is ten o'clock at night, time for the news, every American grabs his remote control and channel-surfs to the nearest news station. A neat-looking blonde woman comes in view of the screen. In a polished manner, she tells us of twenty-five aboveground nuclear explosions that were picked up by our American scientists. She tells us that they are now telling us that there is a 700 percent chance that our lungs are going to be devastated by these blasts. Thank god, a commercial comes on. A sweet young athletic girl comes on and for three minutes describes to us how if we eat ice cream, it will give us stomach cancer. Back to the news. There is a water shortage in America, and all taps will be shut off for at least three days. Then she says that the IRS has caught 5 million tax evaders and they will be hanged at dawn.

Does this sound familiar? I hope not! But some of us seem to think that the world is this bad. We can't change the world by worrying; put it in God's hands. I would like to leave you with this thought the pursuit of joy and happiness is a matter of choice, laugh more, love more, learn to relax more, and most of all, learn to forgive more.

My Good Friend

Ten years after my daughter's death, the world went crazy again. I had a friend that I had meet when I was in grade school and was close to for all of our lives. I sold life insurance. He always told me, "Don't bug me. When I get married, I will buy life insurance from only you."

I never bugged him, and when he got married, he bought a significant amount of insurance as he told me he would. He farmed and ranched north of my hometown. As he got to be a bigger farmer and rancher, his needs changed after each of his five children were born. He added more insurance to himself, then one day he asked me about insurance on his wife. (He always told me that it didn't matter what insurance that he bought because he would always collect more than the money he put in.) I sold him 500,000 of one-year annual renewable term on his wife. I told him that he wouldn't like this policy because next year, the premium would increase, and if he bought a twenty-year term, it would stay the same for all twenty years. He did not want that. Only the cheapest policy at this time. A year later, when the premium increased, he came to me and said, "You were right. I should have taken the twenty-year term."

Now, that is what he wanted. I told him that I would get him a policy, but he would have to drop the annual renewable policy. He said he would just not pay that premium. I said that would be fine. That is the way I applied for the new policy.

My wife and his wife were good friends. She always told my wife if she ever had an accident to make sure the law knew it wouldn't be an accident.

November 17, 1999, our daughter brought twin grandchildren into the world. I had to travel home that evening so that I could work the next day. My wife had stayed with our daughter at the hospital. About one in the morning, I got a call from my wife to tell me that my friend's wife was dead, and the law arrested her husband for her murder. It was hard to believe. About a week before that night, her husband had called me and told me he was going to kill her because she wanted a divorce and would take half his farm. I talked to him for a while and talked him into coming into town and talking with an attorney. I called the attorney and set up an appointment for them. It was to be on the same day that my grand-children were born. They weren't living together at this time, but he had talked her into coming over to their house and going to town together. After they got home, they must have had a confrontation in the garage, and he ended up beating her to death. He then took her body down in the basement and said she slipped and feel down the stairs. God, where are you now? This just took another toll on my issues I was already having with God. I thought that my friend was always a good Christian. I had a hard time believing that he would do this, but I guess I never knew his heart, only the physical person. A week later, he was let out of jail on bail. He called and wanted me to come out and see him. I drove out to his house. It was kind of eerie to go into the house that I have been in many times. He wanted me to call his attorney and tell him how much insurance his wife had. After I talked with his attorney and told him that she had a term policy for 500,000, my friend told me that wasn't right. He said he keep the older policy as well as the new one and also called the company and added accidental death to the policy for an additional 750,000 dollars. After checking with the companies that this was actually true, I called the attorney back to tell him. He went crazy over the news. During the next year and half before the trial, I was interviewed many, many times by DCI agents (Division of Criminal Investigators). It was a year and half of hell just driving more nails in my coffin with God. This was a big story in itself. After many tribulations and disappointments for a year and half, my friend was sentenced to life in prison without parole.

THE MIRACLE

We always believed in God but weren't sure what kind of a god we were believing in after my daughter's death. We were taking care of our twin grandkids one day when the phone rang. My wife answered the phone, and all I heard was "Oh my god, is she okay?"

It was a short conversation. When she hung the phone up, she told our friends that were visiting us that they would have to take care of the twins for a short while until our daughter got home. We had to go to Pierre right away. Our son's daughter, age three, had just been run over, and she was at the hospital. My son told my wife that Shaina would be okay but wanted us to come over. He wanted us to stop by the house and bring her some PJs. Grandma wanted to stop at the Walmart and get her a new set of PJs and a stuffed animal. When we arrived at the hospital, my son met us in the lobby and told us she was not going to be all right. Our granddaughter had, in fact, a very serious condition and may not live. Shaina was getting picked up at the babysitters and ran to the car ahead of the other kids. Her mother had left a pop can on the dash of the car. The car was left running because it was chilly outside, and her mother was just going to run in the babysitter's house and get the kids and go right home. She had gone in, and Shaina had run out to be the first in the car. Shaina was getting in on the driver's side door and grabbed the wheel to help herself. She was reaching for the pop at the same time. The wheel turned, and the car came out of gear, allowing the car to roll backward. Shaina was thrown from the car and landed on her stomach facing the back of the car. The front tire went between her legs and up her back, resting on her body stopping just before her head. Her older sister, Bethany, saw what had happened and ran screaming back to the house to get her mother. Two women were driving around the corner and saw what had happened. They placed a call to 911. My son was an EMT and heard the call come over his radio and knew that the address was that of their babysitter.

He was at the scene in minutes. The women had to make some quick decisions. They couldn't lift the car from Shaina. They decided to drive it off. Her mother got into the car and slowly drove the car off of her daughter. All the blood vessels were ruptured from her legs to the top of her head. She was rushed to the hospital and the doctors were called. Todd told us they initially thought she was going to be fine. After some tests, they discovered her liver and spleen were both broken, and her entire cavity was full of blood and still bleeding. Emergency surgery was required. There were two surgeons involved, and her general doctor was called in to assist. The doctors said all they could do was to try and stop the bleeding and send her to Sioux Falls to a larger facility that could handle these kinds of accidents. They also said that they weren't sure that she would make it through the surgery. Many from the church family gathered in the waiting room and clasped hands for a short prayer. Then everyone dispersed to make calls all over the country to start a prayer chain. I remember my son telling me while choking in tears. That God took his sister and he wasn't going to let him take his daughter.

Time passed by. It was storming outside so the air ambulance couldn't fly. A couple of hours went by and I stepped back in the waiting room. The doctors were there, and everyone including the doctors were crying. I knew this had to be bad. Tears were flowing but not from sadness. The doctors said that they could not explain what had happened. When they opened my granddaughter, there was no blood in the cavity and the liver was damaged but not to the extent that was seen on the CAT scan. The spleen was not damaged as badly as they had seen on the x-ray. We know what happened. God had performed a miracle right before our eyes. My wife went to Sioux Falls with our son. The plane finally flew about three hours past when they thought that they could. My wife said when they got to the hospital, the ER doctor asked them if they would mind if he took pictures of Shaina. He said that he taught emergency training and wanted to have his students see a picture of someone that actually made it through this type of accident.

He said he had never seen anyone in her condition, with all of the broken blood vessels ever live. We didn't tell him we knew it was a miracle.

LIFES DRAMA

What is life worth in small town?

What is life worth in a large city?

What is different in a town of eight hundred population and a city of several million?

Nothing!

The night I came home from the birth of another grandchild was a beautiful fall evening. My wife stayed in Omaha to help our daughter. I got home about 10:30 p.m. and got to bed a little later. In our bedroom at the back of the house, we had a large fan above the bed. We had a glass door that went out to our deck from our bedroom. I woke up shortly after being in bed to what I thought was lighting coming in from the back door, and the fan was shining it all over the room. I got up and looked out the door, and all I could see were bright stars in the sky. I couldn't understand where lighting would be coming from in late October. I decided to go to the front door and see if there was any coming from the front of the house. When I opened the front door, I saw all kinds of cop cars and an ambulance at our neighbors down the end of the street. I saw someone that looked like a fireman walking really fast down the street, sheltering two small children under his coat. I walked to the road to see what was happening, and a woman came running up to me, screaming and crying. She grabbed me and shouted that her sister Pam had been shot, and Pam's husband, Ken, had done it. She continued to run after the children (Ken and Pam's kids). I turned and quickly walked to the end of the block. The sheriff grabbed me and handed me some yellow tape.

"Help get me this crime scene tape up before a ton of people show up."

Crime scene, what in the world is he talking about? This guy (Ken) was the town cop and a good friend of mine. I noticed that the ambulance doors were still open. I was busy putting tape up and did not see the ambulance pull out. They told me that Ken said that he accidently shot his wife. She was shot in the head while sleeping in bed with her youngest child. The DCI (Department of Criminal Investigation) agents had already gotten there. It was starting to be cold outside, and they couldn't seem to get their cell phones working from this side of town. I told them that they could use my house phone from my office in the front of my large garage across the road. I opened it for them and told them to make themselves at home. After that, I walked home and ran into my wife's cousin that lived at the end of the block. She saw me coming home and came over to sit on the front deck to visit for a while. After a while, I called my wife to tell her what was going on, then I went back to bed. The phone rang about 3:30; it was a DCI agent from Sioux Falls. He said one of the agents called him from this number and wondered if I could go find him and ask him to call him back. I got dressed and walked back down the block. I found two agents sitting in a pickup truck, talking to our new states attorney. I found out later that she and Ken had a relationship going on. He had called her before he even called the ambulance. I told the DCI agent to take the conversation inside my shed. I would make some coffee and turn some heat on so they could be more comfortable. They could go ahead and make this their headquarters if they wanted and they did want. I went in and made some coffee and made them some room, and they made it their office for a week and half. They couldn't get cell service, so my phone was tied up for the entire time they were here.

I was mayor of Highmore for a few years. Pam was the city secretary, and Ken was the town cop. I thought I knew them fairly well, but the stories that came out after this night I wasn't sure I knew them at all. I let Ken have a key to my shed and to some of my cars so if he needed to use one he could and he watched my shed for me. A few days into the investigation, an agent came to my door in the early evening and asked if I could come over to the shed so they could visit with me. When I got to the shed, I met an agent that I got to know earlier a few years before this on another case. I got to know Mike Braley when another friend of mine went nuts and killed his wife. Mike said when I walked in the door, "What are you doing here?"

I said they wanted to ask me some questions I suppose.

Mike replied, "You guys don't need to ask him any questions. He doesn't know anything you can't find out by visiting with other people. I'll walk you home."

We left the shed, and he told me, "You really don't want to be involved in another one of these again."

I thanked Mike and we talked for about an hour and caught up on some old times. I came across the yard a few days later. Mike was coming out of Ken's house and hollered at me. "We got him! Haven't you heard us shooting in the house?"

I said, "No." Mike said, "We found the spot he shot from and it couldn't have been and accident."

Three weeks later, Mike died from a medical problem. Later, Ken was found guilty and was sentenced to life without parole. We had never in our town had a murder in over seventy-five years, and in the last fifteen, we have had two. I was involved as a witness in both of them. That is the difference in the size of the cities. You know all of the people. Circumstances don't change.

Our Only Son, Michael Todd Newton

When we lived in Gregory and our son was about two, he traveled with me on the school bus. I drove a bus to make extra income. He loved to be with Dad, and Dad loved to have him along. We always tried to teach him everything from the get-go. He was extremely interested in learning. He walked at eight and half months old. He would pick up his walker and walk so he could move faster. He crawled up on everything while other kids his age and older just sat and watched him. He always wanted to do all things by himself without help.

As time, progressed Todd became ready for a playmate. My wife was pregnant with our second child (Lori). I taught school and drove the bus morning and night for the Gregory school system. We lived in a trailer park east of town and didn't get to meet too many neighbors. It was late on a Friday night and a very chilly December evening. Our friends had just left for home from playing an evening of cards. My wife had started to have child pains, and a couple hours later, we thought she better head to the hospital and have it checked out. Not wanting to wake our son, she said we could call one of the neighbors that she had met. The neighbor told her that she would come and help, day or night. She was all excited when she got to our home (and loud). I told her she needed to settle down or she would wake Todd. I had never met this person before. She had been involved in a car accident, and her face was terribly scarred. It was scary for me, and I knew it would be worse for our son if she woke him. I said I would take my wife to the hospital and be back as soon as I could. I got her to the hospital and called her parents to come and help; they were over two hours away. After about an hour, I thought I should go back and check on Todd. When I got home and pulled up to the house, I noticed our house door was wide open, and my son was sitting on the couch in a very cold living room, crying so hard he was shaking. The neighbor saw me drive up, so she came walking across the yard. Cigarette in one hand and a beer in the other. How long she was gone I didn't know, but I told her to go back where she came from. It took several hours to get Todd to settle down. By morning, my wife's folks had gotten here. I was able to go back to the hospital and meet my new daughter. We thought we were having another boy, so we didn't have a name for a girl. It took us three days to pick a name (Lorinda Lynn Newton); we would call her Lori for short (and not knowing we would have her for nineteen short years). As the kids grew, so did our family. We added four more girls as time went on. Todd was outnumbered five to one but managed to keep his sanity through the years.

We moved several times through the years and decided to move home in the early eighties. We decided we wanted our kids to grow up with grandpas and grandmas and cousins. Something that neither of my wife nor I grew up with. We thought it would be fantastic for the kids to grow up with horses and cattle to work with and make their lives more worthwhile. Fishing and hunting and some golf were the things that took up weekends. The picture below shows one of those times that Todd controlled the situation by not letting his little sister, Brenda, hold the snake they had found. You can see how Brenda handled the situation

As the kids got older, they seemed to enjoy the times we went fishing and hunting. Todd wrote a story for the class in high school about a special time that we all went fishing. He enjoyed these times and especially this time when Lori caught a fish.

The Large-Mouth Bass
by
Michael Todd Newton

This spring, our family converged on a local bass dam surrounded by plenty of trees and bellowing cows. After several unsuccessful attempts to catch the biggest large-mouth that you ever saw, my fifteen-year-old sister decided to attempt her hand at the art of casting. She swung that rod and reel around her head like David taking a shot at Goliath! When she finally had enough motion, she let that string go—that worm, string, and bobber sailed over the trees and landed gently in the water only three feet from the shore! Immediately, the bobber went out of sight, but the line was caught in the trees! In the excitement, my sister started pulling that monster out of the water and straight up into the trees. I quickly assessed the situation—my dad, out of shape, couldn't climb that tree; my mother could give advice but wouldn't touch a fish at any time, not even with a ten-foot pole; our dog wouldn't stop barking; and the other kids wouldn't stop laughing. So I knew it was up to me. With my buck knife in my teeth, I played like Tarzan and started up that tree with enough vigor, Tarzan's mom would have been proud of me. I hung in the tree by my heels out over the water. I looked down at that lake Lunker, and all I could see was twenty pounds of mouth staring back at me! Swinging like a trapeze artist, I managed to cut the lake Lunker free with my buck knife and swing it toward shore. Dad, kids, and dog jumped on it to keep it from wrestling its way back into the water. We were absolutely astounded when we got home and weighed that monster. The fish's body weighed two pounds, and the mouth weighed over thirty pounds! What a day. I will never let my sister forget that day.

"Every Kid has these first"

In every kid's life, there is always a turbulent time, and each has to test their parents at least once. Our son was no different. Todd was a junior in high school. He never went out much; he was content to be at home with the family. He never really needed to go out and drink and smoke with the other kids. Then came a time where he took my pickup and decided to go downtown for the evening. He came home and went to bed, never saying anything about what happened. The next day, we got a call from the sheriff's office. He had gone to school and got Todd out of school, and I was to come to the sheriff's office and pick him up. I wasn't sure what was going on. When I got to the sheriff's office, he told me that our pickup was seen driving across the courthouse lawn the night before leaving some deep tracks in the lawn. I asked Todd why he drove across the lawn, and he told me he didn't. I asked how they knew it was our pickup, and the sheriff had gotten a part from the tail light that was missing and it fit our pickup. When Todd was faced with this, he still denied driving the pickup across the lawn. He said I wasn't driving. I asked was it our pickup and who was driving? He said it was our pickup, but he wasn't driving. Who was? It was the grade school principal's granddaughter. She was a senior, and they were being chased by some other kids. When I asked Todd why he wasn't driving, he said he had a beer and was always told not to drink and drive. He told me the truth. We had to go to court. I was sharing an office with the states attorney. When he got done and they pleaded guilty, the judge asked if anyone had anything to say before he sentenced them. I stood and said, "I did, Your Honor."

Everyone looked at me like I was crazy. "Your Honor, I would like to ask the sheriff and the states attorney one simple question. I know we live in a small town, and we have a beautiful swimming pool. I know that the pool had to be drained twice already this year and sanitized. The reason and everyone knows why. The volunteer fire department after getting drunk at one of their meetings stole a pig and put it in the pool, then after another meeting, they stole one of the other firemen's boat and put it in the pool. Now everyone knows about this, and I would like to know what kind of a sentence each of those people got for what they cost the taxpayer? After all of these incidents the pool had to drained, completely sanitized, refilled with new water and re-heated. These were all business people of the community and names aren't hard to come by."

The judge turned to the sheriff (who was one of them that did the deed) and asked, "Was this true?"

The reluctant sheriff just shook his head that it was true. The judge then turned to the kids and said, "Well, I am going to give these kids something. They will have to do nine hours of community service at the courthouse to help the janitor fix the lawn."

Instead of the twenty-seven hours, I was going to give them. That evening, I received a call from the janitor and she said she already had the lawn fixed, and after hearing what I said in court, she said the kids wouldn't have to come for any work.

TODD'S LIFE

Todd had four children and a wife who, if diagnosed, would have been diagnosed with borderline personality disorder. He worked for the state of South Dakota in the computer department. He was also a volunteer for the Pierre, South Dakota, fire department. He also worked at Walmart in his spare time to help provide for his family. Todd was a great father and husband and did everything around the house with the kids because his wife wouldn't. Todd loved to be in the outdoors. He grew up working on the farm for his grandparents during the summers. I was gone a lot more than I should have been, trying to build an insurance agency that would provide us a living.

During track practice one day, Todd was trying to pole vault. During one vault, he got up in the air about eight to nine feet and then fell backward. When he fell, he severely broke his arm in many places. I met them at the hospital. My wife had gotten him to a small-town hospital, but he needed a specialist, and we had to take him to a larger hospital. After surgery, I guess his track days were over.

I always loved to take my son hunting and fishing. He was a terrific sportsman. He was certainly a better shot than I was. I had a friend, Mike Ferris, who gave me a gun for my son to use when he was sick. Todd wanted to hunt deer. He used Mike's gun, and we let him shoot from the pickup. He shot all of our deer that season. His cousin helped clean all of them. This was the last season Todd would ever hunt.

I remember when Todd became an EMT on the fire department. He was called to his first car accident, and it was a horrible accident. A car had run head on into a semi-truck at sixty miles an hour. This was Todd's first accident, and it took the fire department and EMTs and several weeks for him to be able to handle this.

Todd and Mom and Dad bought a boat together and decided to leave it at Todd's since he lived very close to the Missouri River. He was able to take his friends and family out whenever he could, which he tried several times a week.

Todd could fix about anything. He especially enjoyed making race cars for derby racing for scouts. He helped his son build these cars and somehow always seem to get him first place.

Problem Diagnosed

In early September of 2009, all the kids were at our house for dinner. I had made some homemade wine and wanted each to just have a taste of what I had done. Todd told me that he was sorry, but he hurt so bad in his stomach that he couldn't taste anything, but he couldn't eat as well. They left early to go home. Todd told us that he had been doctoring for prostrate problems for over a year. That was the first time we even knew that he wasn't feeling well. I told my wife that I think that he was a little young to have prostrate problems. She agreed. The next day, I happened to be in the Pierre area. I received a call from a surgeon at the Pierre hospital. He told me that Todd had come in that morning with a terrific pain in his stomach, and they had done a CAT scan and found a mass in his stomach area and were taking him in for immediate surgery, and Todd wanted us to know. I called my wife and told her she should get to Pierre as soon as she could. We also found out that the current doctor that was taking care of him actually used a microwave procedure on him because of his prostrate. He just never went the extra mile to find out what was actually wrong with him. After six hours of surgery, they took a good part of his large intestine and parts of his small intestine, sixteen lymph nodes, and a large mass outside of his intestines. The surgeon would not tell us that it was cancer until after the tests had come back from the lab. He knew full well that it was and that came across to us as well. After the tests came back, he was told he had colon cancer and had traveled to his liver and several of his other organs. Why, Lord? Why had the doctor not taken any more tests? If they had caught it early enough, our son might still be alive.

WOW!

After Todd got out of the hospital, we were sitting in Burger King in Pierre with everyone having supper. Todd was on the phone with his cousin in Utah. We had been talking to him about going to a cancer center in Houston, Texas. We said that we would take care of his children and pay for him and his wife to travel there and find out if there was anything that they might be able to do that they couldn't do in small time hospital in Pierre, South Dakota. While he was on the phone, his wife came over to our table and stood in front of us and yelled at the top of her lungs for everyone in Burger King to hear what she was saying. My wife and I will never in our lifetime forget the words that came out of her mouth.

"He is not going anywhere. He is not going to disrupt our lives just to save his life."

We couldn't believe what we were hearing. She kept yelling and screaming, so I got up and ushered her outside as she screamed all the way. When we got outside, Todd met us and calmly said, "Dad, it is all right. We will go home and talk about all of this and make a decision on what we should do."

In response to this, everything went downhill at a rapid pace. When we talked to him about Texas, she evidently won the argument. He came back with the fact that Pierre had some of the best doctors in the world, and now they had a great oncologist that had just moved from Sioux Falls to Pierre, a lot smaller hospital. We did some research on him and found out that he had been asked to leave

Sioux Falls (too late, we think he was one of the worst and did not stay in Pierre long either). My wife did a tremendous amount of research on colon cancer and felt like we needed a second opinion. That was stopped short.

LAST CHRISTMAS AND HOLIDAY

Time went by quickly, and we were going to have all of the kids come home for the holidays. We were thinking that this could very well be the last Christmas that we would have Todd to be able to celebrate with us. Once again, we were pretty disappointed that Todd's wife insisted that they go to her mother's place for the holidays, as they always had. We did not know at the time that her mother intended to leave on a trip to Europe Christmas day so she wouldn't be there for Christmas anyway. Only after she left for her trip was Todd allowed to leave and come to spend some time with us. Todd did not feel well but drove the four hundred miles on terrible snowy roads and in a blizzard so he could be with his siblings and parents for the rest of Christmas. It took its toll on his health and also on us as a family.

During the holidays, Todd decided that it would be nice to celebrate New Year's in Rapid City and go to the lighting ceremony at the mountain carving at Crazy Horse. We took almost all of our children and grandchildren. Twenty-three people. We bought rooms for all and went to New Year's supper at the Crazy Horse Memorial south of Rapid City. The lighting ceremony was a joke. They had a small window that we were to look through and a Christmas tree light that shone through the window. It would rotate and show different colors on the window, like lighting on a Christmas tree. Dinner was either steaks for $27 or a pizza buffet for $5. It was a choice between $800 and $150; we decided on the buffet. However, Todd's wife wanted steak, and she became extremely angry when I told her she would have to eat what everyone else ate. She ran out to the car, crying, and that just ruined the night for Todd and all of his family. We just let her go. When we got back to the motel and were watching television, she was pouting in her room and only came down to our room where everyone else was to celebrate the turning of the New Year, then right back to her room. It could have been a lot happier New Year. We knew it was probably Todd's last New Year; why would she make it harder?

FIRST OF YEAR 2010

After Christmas, things started out with Todd taking chemotherapy; there was no more discussion of him going to any other cancer center. His wife had convinced him that the oncologist that moved from Sioux Falls, South Dakota, to Pierre to become the oncologist in this small town was the best in the world. We didn't know at the time that he was ask to leave Sioux Falls because of some problems. Needless to say, we were not overjoyed with his attitude and performance.

We had a trip planned for several months to South Africa on a farm tour before we knew that Todd would become sick. When we told Todd we would cancel the trip, he would have nothing to do with it. He said that he would be fine until we got home and would enjoy looking at all of the pictures. We made sure we had the right kind of cell phones so we could stay in contact with him while we were gone. We were gone for two weeks. He did enjoy the pictures when we got home, but his health was starting to deteriorate more rapidly. His home was not cohesive enough to meet his needs, and there was no one there that really wanted to take care of him. His surgeon wanted him to go into hospice at the hospital. They gave him a two-room suite with a couch and chairs in the second room with a refrigerator. Visitors could come and go without disturbing his family at the hospital; we were told that his wife did not want us to be there with him. A nurse friend of Todd's came and told us that she informed his wife that there was no way that she was going to keep us from seeing our son. Todd did not want us to stay away. We had a motorhome and made a deal with the state of South Dakota that we could park in their state park even though it was not open yet. That way, we would be able to go to the hospital on a daily basis, and my wife could help with the grandkids.

Todd was captain of one of the ladder companies for the Pierre Fire Department; one day, a member of the department came to see Todd. He had on his dress uniform. He asked Todd to accompany him to the window looking toward the street below. When Todd looked out of the window, his ladder company was on the street next to the ladder truck all in their dress uniforms and standing at attention. When Todd looked out, they all saluted and turned the siren and the lights on in the truck. This was extremely emotional and brought a flood of tears to everyone's eyes.

COLORED LIGHTS

One day, Todd called myself and my wife into his room. He wanted to ask us a question. He said, "When people walk into my room, I see a colored light above their head. Some of them have green lights, some of them red, and a few of them have black. I have no idea what that means. Is God trying to tell me something? I'm wondering if God is trying to get me to reach them and tell them about Jesus Christ?"

He specifically mentioned his sister, Monica. He said that he knew she was going to be all right because she had a different-colored light. He said he didn't know if God was trying to tell him to pray for these people or try to reach them in different ways. He said he didn't know what was happening and neither did we.

Some of the incidents that have bothered in the years that followed my father's death and the death of our daughter still tend to haunt me today. When my father was dying, he looked over in the corner of the room and said, "Jesus, who are those other guys with you?" It was only a day later when he passed away.

After my daughter died, we had three different people tell us that Lori came to their bedside and sat to talk with them. Her sister said the next morning that Lori and her cousin Laura (who died from cancer when she was only three) both came. Lori told her she had forgotten something but did not tell her what it was. Lori's cousin, Jennifer, called us sometime later and told us the exact same thing, except she did not say that Laura was with her.

Several months later, Lori's softball coach gave my wife a call and told us that Lori had come to her and sat on the side of the bed and talked with her and told her she was all right even after the things that happened to her. But she never said what things. Each year on Lori's date of her death, these three people always call us because of what happened.

WHY, LORD?

Why, Lord? How many times in twenty-four hours do we ask ourselves this question? Knowing that we will not get an answer until the day that we meet the Lord and ask him why?

Why would any loving God allow our daughter at age nineteen to be killed and our son of forty-one to suffer and die in an unbearable circumstance? Why would he put our family through two murders of wives of our friends? The almost loss of a granddaughter getting ran over with a car and a grandson born with seizures?

Todd never complained. At first, he was angry, but after he accepted his fate (he did much better than Mom and Dad), he got busy and wanted to help everyone else. He wanted them to learn what he knew about Jesus Christ and our way to heaven. I couldn't reason why a god who supposedly loved everyone would do this to my family. I hated God. I really didn't want to have anything to do with him. I kept God as far from me as I could. He told his uncle who always valued money more than relationships that he should get right with God. He told him it didn't matter what money or physical items that you collected on earth. How big your house was, the kind of car you drove, or what other items you cherished. What really mattered when you get in the situation that he was in that you loved our Lord and Savior. What mattered to him was that he had a real personal relationship with Jesus Christ.

Todd said, "You aren't going to take anything with you, your family, your friends, your possessions or your wealth. All you can take is your relationship with Jesus Christ."

We felt good that he was still trying to reach other people but certainly did not understand how he could be reaching out to the god that we knew. How could the god that he was reaching and teaching about do this to our son and our family? Why was God putting his family and ours through this dismal disaster?

GRANDPA THE THIEF

One day, Todd wanted to talk with me about how he was going to leave his family, so they could have something to live on. He had talked to his friend, John, who worked for the attorney general's office at the state government. John told him he should consider a family trust. I assured him that I thought that was a good idea. John could not do the work for him to set one up, so I suggested an attorney that had done work for me in the past. My attorney friend told me that he was retiring but would introduce Todd to a new attorney that his office had hired to take his place. When they met with Todd, they told him it would be great if he would use his insurance and retirement money to fund the trust and give his family and kids some money to live on and use for school. after the trust was signed and the bank was selected. His nine-year-old son came screaming and crying from his hospital room. He was screaming that I (Grandpa) had stolen all of their money, and they wouldn't be able to go and vacation in Europe and be able to buy new cars for each of the kids, like his mother had been telling them. She had promised that when our son died that they would be able to go all of these exotic places. I am not sure what all she had told them, but do know that they would not of had any money to live on if she had gotten her way.

GRANDPA THE THIEF #2

Things were going downhill rather rapidly. My wife's sister called and wanted to bring my wife's mother to see Todd. Her siblings had taken her to Sioux Falls to a nursing home. She had a stroke, and they were afraid that I would steal her money. They assumed that she was getting too old to handle her own affairs and did not want my wife (who had taken care of her mother most of her life) and I would not handle things as they wanted. They thought that I stole her money from the farm sale. Her mother had come to me after the sale and said she wanted two things. First, she did not want to put her money in the local bank, and she would like to have life insurance and long-term care insurance so she would not have to depend on anyone to take care of her. I talked to her about an insurance policy that would cover her for life insurance and nursing home in one policy. If she didn't use the life insurance, she would have it for nursing coverage. We put a single premium on a 200,000-life policy that would pay her 4 percent of the 200,000/per month if she had to go to a nursing home. Then I took the 200,000 cash from the sale and put it into an annuity that paid an annual percentage of six and compounded each year.

When she died, the life insurance had been used to pay for all of her nursing home charges, and annuity was split between all eight children. They did not have to sell or touch the land she owned in any way. They could have saved the family a lot of trouble if they would have only asked me what was going on instead of guessing and thinking I was a thief. Our son had worked almost every summer while he was in school for his grandparents. What really bothered my wife and I was when my mother-in-law told my wife that she really didn't need to see Todd. She just thought that he might want to see her before he died. One more form of devastation.

ONE MORE TIME

About a week before our son died, his wife stood at the end of his bed and screamed so the entire hospital could hear.

"You were supposed to be dead two weeks ago. I am getting sick and tired of being up here every day."

That totally devastated our son, my wife, myself, and a lot of other people at the hospital. How could anyone in their right mind stand there and scream that to a dying spouse? We were sickened by her actions and reactions. We were not sure how he put up with her as long as he had. Our son was made of steel and was a man with a great character. After his death, his wife was causing a lot of problems with the children. She threatened suicide and actually left them for a three-day period. We asked her to go to the minister with us and see if we could reconcile some differences or we couldn't and wouldn't be a part of her life. When the minister questioned her about what she had said and done, she absolutely denied she even said or thought those things. Many people at the hospital heard and saw what she had done and confronted us with it later. We decided that we would love and welcome the kids anytime but could not allow her to be part of our lives.

LAST BREATH

I am not sure why God is treating us this way? Todd was always upbeat during his stay in the hospital. Much, much more than I was or ever could have been. I admired and loved my son without reservations. When we were at his room in the hospital, we had to tiptoe around his room like walking on eggshells. We did not want to upset his wife. A lot of Todd's friends came by on a daily basis. John, a friend of Todd's from church, would come by every day, sometimes twice a day. He and Todd would talk, then John would read the Bible to Todd. Todd wanted John to speak at his funeral and tell people certain things that Todd wanted people to know about God. John would sometimes take his entire noon hour and sometimes come back after work. One day after John left, Todd's wife and doctor decided he had been in enough pain and decided to up Todd's morphine intake. He knew and we knew what was going to happen. Todd called in his family and told them that they would cry for a while but wanted them to live a happy life. He also told his sisters and his mother and myself, he appreciated that we had always been there for him. My wife and I had been in this same position with parents and friends of ours. Todd's minister was there and said some prayers. Todd sat up in bed and shook his hand and told him good-bye. The minister said there was a lot of strength in that handshake, and he would be back later that day to see him. He commented one more time that the handshake was really muscular and he was not that weak.

Some of Todd's siblings were there to share with us. After the minister left, the morphine was kicking in and he wanted to lie back down. I moved to the other side of the bed and held his hand and told him for the last time how much I loved him. All he said was "I know, Dad." My wife came over beside him and took her turn holding him and telling him she loved him and cried some with him. I hadn't been able to tell him how much I loved him for a long time. Today, I make sure that the people I love I tell them as often as I can even my friends. We moved to the other side of the bed and let his siblings talk with him and hold him. His sister that was a physician assistant was the last to hold him and tell him how much she loved him when he took his last breath. He was extremely yellow from the cancer killing his liver. It was devastating and almost unbearable to watch him go through this pain and misery. I was, if I could say, extra proud of him as he went through all of this with more grace and dignity than I could have ever mustered.

ANOTHER FUNERAL

The funeral took place in the community Bible church that Todd and his family attended for several years.

The Pierre Fire Department had asked if they could be part of the service. They told Todd they would like to give him a chief's burial even though he was only a captain. They wanted him buried in the fire department's plots at the cemetery. Todd was totally in agreement and proud of what they asked of him. He had told us that he had been a part of several of these services. He knew exactly what would take place. We had no idea what to expect. They had a certain plot in the cemetery where they wanted people of rank in the fire department to be buried. At the church for the viewing, and at the funeral, they had three firemen in their dress uniform guarding the casket the entire time. The night before was the family service and viewing. Anyone was welcome to come, and come they did. Between the two services, they estimated over 1,500 people came through the church. The firemen numbered over 100 members all in their dress uniforms. They were all honor casket bearers and took up almost one section of the church. We had no idea how many lives our son had touched. The service was something that my wife and I will never forget. After the service, the fire department, ambulances, and police department had every side street blocked with vehicles and were all beside them in full salute. As we turned to the road to the cemetery, the ladder company that our son was captain of had their two ladder trucks on each side of the road with their ladders extended across the road draped in black cloth that you had to drive your vehicle under to get into the main gate. At the grave site, the firemen gave their own rites and played taps. (I have never liked the sound of taps.) I know what it stands for and lost friends in war. The minister did a great job with the readings and the Lord's Prayer, I think. I was so stunned I didn't really pay much attention to what was happening.

Todd Newton
(March 19, 1968 - May 8, 2010)

Todd Newton, 42 of Pierre, died on Saturday, May 8 at St. Mary's Hospital in Pierre. Visitation will be from 5:00-7:00PM, Thursday, May 13 at Community Bible Church with a Prayer Service at 7:00PM. Services will be at 10:00AM, Friday, May 14 at Community Bible Church with Burial at Riverside Cemetery in Pierre

Michael "Todd" Newton was born on March 19, 1968 in Huron, SD to Michael and Donna Jean (Hamlin) Newton. Todd attended Highmore High School in Highmore, SD where he was proud to have been on a regular season undefeated football team. Todd graduated high school in 1986 and went on to attend Moorhead State University in Moorhead, MN where he received his BS in Business Administration and Marketing and his AS at Moorhead Technical College in Information Systems/Technology.

While attending college in Moorhead, he met his wife Laura Lee Bruggeman of Mahnomen, MN. They were married on June 22, 1992 in Mahnomen, MN. To this union four children were born, Danielle Jean (18), Bethany LeAnn (15), Shaina Lynn (12), and Travis William (9). They moved to Pierre, SD in 1994 where they have lived and raised their family with strong Christian values and have been an active part of Community Bible Church. With excitement for faith, life and an attitude of excellence, Todd added an irreplaceable light in all of our lives. Todd has always had a love for the outdoors whether it was hunting, fishing, sledding, firework shows or water sports, we could count on Todd to get everyone out enjoying it.

Todd had a special love for helping, fixing, and teaching all he came in contact with. He carried this on coupled with excellence into a part time career of being and EMT, Volunteer Firefighter, and a part of the Search and Rescue team for 9 years. Todd also was very involved with his family and all of their activities. He was very active in Junior Shooting sports, not only while living in Pierre, but for many years prior fixing guns, organizing matches and coaching his children. He enjoyed boy scouts and Boy Scout outings with his son Travis, watching all of his children's plays, concerts, and sports. Todd was also very active in all church activities. Todd was in particular an expert in making winning cars for the Awana derbies.

THANK YOU, JOHN

A great Christian friend of Todd's spoke at my son's funeral. He was kind enough to give me his notes on his speech. He had saved them for all of these years. The following notes are what our son wanted people to know about his death.

These words speak volumes to me today. Thank you, my son and John.

To many of you, Todd is known by different names:

To some, he is a:

Friend

BIT coworker

Pierre Shooters coach

Fireman

Nephew

Cousin

Husband

Father

Son

Brother

Brother-in-law

To me and many others here, he was a brother in Christ. All of those have great meaning to him, but his most treasured title is Child of God.

We are all here to remember a man who was important in our life in at least one of those capacities. Let's all take a moment right now and enjoy a memory of Todd's positive influence in our life.

Todd conveyed a couple messages he wanted shared to his friends. It is my hope that I faithfully fulfill his request.

One of those messages I want to share with you what Todd wanted to make sure everyone knew. How much he appreciated your friendship and kindness that was shown him and his family while in health but especially during his battle with cancer.

- The firefighters: pancake breakfast fund-raiser
- I am sure most of you were at the Pizza Ranch fund-raiser: if you were not, it is most likely because you started to drive and saw that there was nowhere to park and the line steadily extended out the door
- Those at work
- The gracious gift from his church
- The visits at home
- The construction and lawn work
- The visits at the hospital (the list goes on and on)
- He truly appreciated all that you did

That was Todd's message to you. but we all have our own message to Todd of his kindness in our lives.

- I can think of the year did not have a trailer to haul close to fifty some people's equipment for their relief and mission work in Mexico. Todd found out about it, came up to me, and said, "I can fix that." He took Mike's trailer.
- Chuck Hanson that after Todd's passing from this life, when he was back home, he started looking around, and he saw Todd's fingerprints everywhere in his house.

1. The dog kennel backyard.
2. Step on our deck is Todd's work.
3. Electric outlet in the living room.

4. Computer upgrade and helped with the wireless network.
5. Plumbing for a water line to the fridge for the ice maker.
6. The boarder on the living room wall was done with the help of Todd and Laura.
7. The day he installed the dishwasher after helping tilled under the entire backyard, leveled it, planted seed, and set up the sprinklers.
8. Todd repaired the wall in the downstairs bathroom after Hannah unsuccessfully tried doing chin-ups on the towel bar.
9. Todd was always available with his pickup and trailer for hauling kennel panels, power seeders, and lawn aerators to the house, plus tree branches, rubble, and old furniture to the dump (think that was actually be Mike's).

These are the same attributes of a life well lived.

Work Story

Brian Oakland wrote:

I had a working relationship with Todd for thirteen years, starting out as green as a computer support technician could be. A lot of the things I learned early on I learned by following Todd around and watching him solve all kinds of problems, many of which most others were just unable to figure out. In fact, he was so knowledgeable about what he did that he was the only technician authorized to solve the Big Boss's computer problems, no matter how simple or how complex. That says a lot about the professional demeanor he always carried as well.

As for me, there is one thing about firefighters and other emergency responders that I admire most, and that is the human quality that allows a man to put his life before the lives of others. Some people have that quality, and some don't. "Better me than you," someone of that character might say. Todd was stricken with a condition that no person should ever have to go through, and privately, there may have been many chances for him to ask, "Why me?" But publicly, in the last eight short months, Todd displayed that firefighter's courage, essentially putting his life before ours, telling us all, in not so many words, "Better me than you."

These are the same attributes of a life well lived.

I as many of you spent time with Todd the last couple weeks he was in the hospital

Life of courage, one said he has left a legacy of courage.

These are attributes of a life well lived. But Todd had a second message that he wanted me to tell you: that his life was not good enough based on the things he has done. We all have regrets, failures in our life; unfortunately, some are not willing to own up to them.

THE GOSPEL MESSAGE

Jesus states in the Bible that every single person is guilty of sin, which is punished by receiving eternal judgment in the fires of hell. Jesus preached that the only way to escape from hell is to "repent and believe in the gospel." (Mark 1:15)

To repent means to turn from your sins and forsake them by the power of God.

To believe the gospel means that one who is "born again" by the Spirit of God (John 3:3–8) will:

> Believe in Jesus Christ as Almighty God, who is without sin;
>
> Believe in Jesus's sacrificial death on the cross as the only and complete payment for your sins;
>
> Believe in Jesus's bodily resurrection from the dead on the third day;
>
> Believe in Jesus as Lord over all things and confesses this fact to others.

It is that straightforward. It has nothing to do with your righteousness, good works, or engaging in a religious ceremony or cleaning yourself up first to win God's acceptance. If you reject God's loving gift of forgiveness in Jesus Christ, you remain a guilty sinner, waiting to be punished in eternal hell. The Bible says in John 3:36,

"He who believes in the Son has eternal life; but he who does not obey the Son will not see life, but the wrath of God abides on him."

He was forgiven; now you know why Todd was good enough!

Closing:

> What cancer can't do!
> It cannot cripple love.
> It cannot shatter hope.
> It cannot corrode faith.
> It cannot destroy peace.
> It cannot kill friendships.
> It cannot suppress memories.
> It cannot silence courage.
> It cannot invade the soul.
> It cannot steal eternal life.
> It cannot conquer the Spirit.
>
> Anonymous

Thank You, Jessica and Kari

A person that had rented an apartment from us in Pierre found out that we were the parents of Todd Newton. She worked at the government where our son worked. She told us that one of his coworkers, Kari Stulken, said she had an e-mail from Todd that she kept for all of these years on her phone and was kind enough to share it with us. The following is the e-mail sent to Kari Stulken on March 31, 2010, from our son.

From: Gebert, Jessica
Jessica.Gebert@state.sd.us
Subject: FW: chapter coming to a close
Date: Marl, 2017, 1:36:30 PM
To: mnewton4666@gmail.com

Hi, Donna,

Here is the e-mail my boss, Kari Stulken, has kept in her inbox after all these years.

God bless.

From: Stulken, Kari
Sent: Wednesday, March 01, 2017 1:24 PM
To: Gebert, Jessica
Subject: FW: chapter coming to a close

From: Newton, Todd
Sent: Wednesday, March 31, 2010 12:14 PM
To: Newton, Todd
Subject: chapter coming to a close

It has been a pleasure working with many of you. I have had a unique opportunity to get to know some of you better than others, as some of you already know, I have been diagnosed with terminal colon cancer. The cancer that I have is one that about 40 percent get which has the KRAS mutation for which there is no cure.

So while I am still able to write everyone a note, I figured that this would be a good time as I will be spending more time at home. Please feel free to send e-mails and notes to me at nutonian@pie. midco.net and you can find me on Facebook under the same address, my wife also set up a www.caringbridge.org/visit/toddnewton site that you can also get better updates as my wife is writing those.

As I will be less attentive to the phone calls and e-mail, please make sure to include Roger.reed@state.sd.us, Jeremy.shultz@state. sd.us, or Dale.luckhurt@stae.sd.us for future requests.

Thanks for all your prayers and support through this whole process. They have really meant a lot to me and my family.

Todd Newton
Technology Integration Specialist
State of South Dakota

WITH THE LORD'S HELP, THIS KEEPS US GOING
THE RACE

I
"Quit! Give up! You're beaten!"
They shout out and plead.
"There's just too much against you now.
This time you can't succeed!"
And as I start to hang my head
In front of failure's face,
My downward fall is broken by
The memory of a race.
And hope refills my weakened will
As I recall that scene;
For just the thought of that short race
Rejuvenates my being.

II
A children's race—young boys, young men;
How I remember well.
Excitement, sure, but also fear;
It wasn't hard to tell.
They all lined up so full of hope:
Each thought to win that race.

Or tie for first, or if not that,
At least take second place.
And fathers watched from off the side,
Each cheering for his son.
And each boy hoped to show his dad
That he would be the one.
The whistle blew and off they went!
Young hearts and hopes afire.
To win, to be the hero there
Was each young boy's desire.
And one boy in particular
Whose dad was in the crowd,
Was running near the lead and thought,
"My dad will be so proud."
But as he speeded down the field
Across a shallow dip,
The little boy who thought to win,
Lost his step and slipped.
Trying hard to catch himself
His hands flew out to brace,
And mid the laughter of the crowd
He fell flat on his face.
So down he fell and with him hope
He couldn't win it now'—
Embarrassed, sad, he only wished
To disappear somehow'.
But as he fell his dad stood up
And showed his anxious face,
Which to the boy so clearly said:
"Get up and win the race!"
He quickly rose, no damage done
Behind a bit, that's all—
And ran with all his mind and might
To make up for his fall.
So anxious to restore himself
To catch up and to win

His mind went faster than his legs;
He slipped and fell again!
He wished that he had quit before
With only one disgrace.
"I'm hopeless as a runner now;
I shouldn't try to race."
But in the laughing crowd he searched
And found his father's face.
That steady look which said again:
"Get up and win the race!"
So, he jumped up to try again.
Ten yards behind the last—
"If I'm to gain those yards/' he thought,
"I've got to move real fast."
Exerting everything he had,
He gained eight or ten,
But trying so hard to catch the lead
He slipped and fell again!
Defeat! He lay there silently
A tear dropped from his eye—
"There's no sense running anymore:
Three strikes I'm out, why try?"
The will to rise had disappeared
All hope had fled away;
So far behind, so error-prone:
A loser all the way.
"I've lost, so what's the use," he thought.
"Til live with my disgrace."
But then he thought about his dad
Who soon he'd have to face.
"Get up," an echo sounded low.
"Get up and take your place.
You were not meant for failure here.
Get up and win the race."
With borrowed will,
"Get up," it said,

"You haven't lost at all,
For winning is not more than this:
To rise each time, you fall."
So up he rose to win once more,
And with a new commit
He resolved that win or lose,
At least he wouldn't quit.
So far behind the others now.
The most he'd ever been—
Still he gave it all he had
And ran as though to win.
Three times he'd fallen stumbling:
Three times he'd rose again.
Too far behind to hope to win
He still ran to the end.
They cheered the winning runner
As he crossed first place,
Head high and proud and happy;
No falling, no disgrace.
But when the fallen youngster
Crossed the line, last place,
The crowd gave him the greater cheer
For finishing the race.
And even though he came in last
With head bowed low, unproud,
You would have thought he won the
Race to listen to the crowd.
And to his dad he sadly said,
"I didn't do so well."
"To me you won," his father said.
"You rose each time you fell."

III
And when things seem dark and hard
And difficult to face,
The memory of that little boy
Helps me in my race.
For all of life is like that race.
With ups and downs and all.
And all you have to do to win
Is rise each time you fall.
"Quit!" "Give up, you're beaten!"
They still shout in my face.
But another voice within me says:
"Get up and win the race!"

Author Unknown

FAITH RESTORED

10,220 Days Later

Please don't ask me if I am over it yet.
I'll never be "over it"
Please don't tell me they are in a better place.
They aren't here.
Please don't say, "At least they aren't suffering."
I haven't come to terms why they had to suffer at all.
Please don't tell you know how I feel,
Unless you have lost a child.
Please don't tell me to go on with my life.
I'm still here, you notice.
Please don't ask me if I feel better.
Losing children isn't a condition that clears up.
Please don't tell me, "God doesn't make mistakes."
You mean, God did this on purpose?
Please don't tell me God never gives you more than you can bear.
Who decides how much another person can bear?
Please just tell me you are sorry.
Please just say you remember if you do.
Please just let me talk if I want to.
Please just let me cry when I must.
Author unknown
At least after 10,220 days, I can say God is still by my side.

After our son died, May 2010, we really haven't gotten back to organized church. I listen to Joel Olsten while I am driving down the road. I realize that good things can come from a broken heart. It is difficult to get back in the spirit, but I realize that other people have as many hurts and sometimes worse than we have. We have four beautiful daughters and thirteen terrific grandchildren that God has allowed us to spoil. This year, I was totally honored when one of my son's daughters ask me to walk her down the aisle for her wedding. It has been more than difficult at times, but we are trying to put God first in our lives. It was totally amazing to read today that President Trump's campaign manager, Kelly Ann Conway, revealed her faith in Jesus Christ. She said it was because of Jesus Christ that put Donald Trump in the White House. She gave Jesus all of the credit for getting her boss elected as the forty-fifth president of the United States of America.

Death is something that we, and most people, don't understand. I have learned whether you are aware of it or not, you view the world through your own perspectives, attitudes, and experiences on your way to adulthood and old age. Good, bad, right or wrong, fair or unfair, your decisions are based on those attitudes. You have the power to adjust or change your attitudes if what you are doing is wrong for your life. We still keep those thoughts somewhere close in the front of our minds. Whether it is financial, health, or the loss of loved ones (especially two children) as we have experienced. We all carry our burdens (our attitudes). What I have really learned as I get older is that time-tested truth that we have absolutely no control over what happens to me or my family in life. I do however have absolute control over how I react to what happens with these burdens. We choose the right perspective and attitude; the path we take will allow us to rise above whatever challenge faces us if we do not leave God out of the equation. We have to have faith in ourselves, our loved ones, and most of all, in our God. With this attitude, we can get busy getting to work helping other people. We need to make the world a better place to live, and don't ever quit.

It has taken the loss of two children, a near-fatal accident with a grandchild, and the loss of the wives murdered by two of my friends, and of course, 10,220 days from the death of our daughter to realize that God never left my side, I left God's side. We raised our children believing and serving the Lord. I left the Catholic faith when my wife and I got married because the priest would not answer the questions I ask him. I told him that we wanted to get married and asked him if he would be a part of the ceremony. He told me that if I got married to a non-Catholic, I would be excommunicated and would go to hell. My dad was with us, and he was also astonished at the answer. He said, "I grew up a non-Catholic, and you two can do whatever you decide and I will still love and support you."

I then went to my wife's pastor and asked him the same questions. He told me, "I think the best way to answer your concerns and questions is to see what Jesus said about them in the Bible."

He opened the Bible and read the answers to my questions. What a revelation. I had never read the Bible. Then I realized that just about anything you wanted to know is in that book. I joined my wife's church to the dismay of my family, except for my dad. My dad was raised in many faiths but was a Christian in every way. My wife's church was a Bible-based church. Over the years, I became a deacon and then an elder before the death of my daughter. I even preached some sermons when they needed someone to fill in. After my daughter's death, I couldn't understand what God was doing to myself and our family. It was extremely difficult to visit with my wife that first year after Lori died. I didn't want to speak of my daughter because my wife would feel hurt. My wife did not want to bring her up to me because she knew that I would feel hurt. A friend of mine that I talked with regularly finally told me to go home and have a heart-to-heart with my wife. That night, I told her I wanted to sit in the hot tub only with her. We talked for about four hours. We came to an understanding why we weren't talking with each other. That evening made the complete difference in our relationship and in our children's. I doubt very much that we would have survived the heartaches and turbulent times we have faced since in our lives if we hadn't talked that night.

We have faced really hard times since and will continue to face the challenges of life with each other and God's help. This book was extremely hard to write at times, but I want people that have faced these times to understand that there is hope and the hope is Jesus Christ, our Lord and Savior. Our family has traveled a broken road. God got lost in the forest several times along the way. I would have loved to dance the first dance at my daughter's (Lori's) wedding, it would have been dancing with one of my five princesses. It has been a long time now; I just have to dream of dancing anytime with my angel. I can see her in my dreams through tears running down my cheeks. The dance would be smooth, the clouds would be dark, but the heavens would be bright and shining with my angel's smile.

I dream of hunting huge deer with my son. I loved being with him in the fields his children and his friends wanting to be along. I can only dream. I realize that while the kids were home I might not have done everything that I should have done. Be a better dad, father, grandfather. Memories are valuable to everyone. They give us strength, keep us going, they give us stories to share with loved ones. We recall some of these times with devotion, tenderness, and a lot of emotions. Most of these reflections are short periods of our short lives with our loved ones. This is the same with God. It took a long time to realize that the Lord never got lost in the woods. That was me being lost, and it feels terrible until you realize what my son wanted me to know about God.

FOOTPRINTS

One night a man had a dream he dreamed he was walking along the beach with the Lord. Across the sky flashed scenes from his life. For each scene, he noticed two sets of footprints in the sand; one belonging to him, and the other to the Lord.

When the last scene of his life flashed before him, he looked back at the footprints in the sand. He noticed that many times along the path of his life there was only one set of footprints, he also noticed that it happened at the very lowest and saddest times in his life.

This really bothered him and he questioned the Lord about it. "Lord, you said that once I decided to follow you, you'd walk with me all the way, but I noticed that during the most troublesome times in my life there is only one set of footprints. I don't understand why when I needed you the most you would leave me."

The Lord replied, "My son, my precious child, I love you and I would never leave you. During your times of trial and suffering, when you see only one set of footprints, it was then that I carried you."

Author unknown

We may still face many problems in the future that the heart hopefully will be strong enough to cope with. Grief plays no favorites. It plays no favorites and ignores all of the rules that preachers, family, friends, and society think that we need to follow. I was told by a preacher three weeks after my daughter's death that he thought that I had grieved enough and to get my checkbook out and buy a memorial gift in her name for the church, like a new piano or organ. After death, the grieving clock sometimes does not stop for a long period. The wounds of the heart don't seem to heal over, and sometimes, the scars are opened and the scabs come off and the tears start to flow when least expected. If you can't control your innermost feelings, attitudes, and beliefs, your wounds will never scar over. I am now allowing Christ to come back to my life. He is the only way that I can control my scars from breaking open. I have found that you cannot count on other human beings to live by on a daily basis. God controls the day and night and controls everything we do. We came from dust, and to dust, we are going to return. We don't have any idea when that is going to happen. We have no idea what God has planned for us because we can't understand his intentions, methods, and decisions.

My son and daughter taught me many valuable lessons in life. Not only was their faith carved in stone, they bore out that faith until the Lord took them to be with him. They taught me no one is perfect in the eyes of the Lord. Perfection is only attained from God through belief in his son, Jesus Christ. This took several years for me to come back to my faith. One of the most important promises God made to his people was that he would send a "messiah," an "anointed one" to cleanse us from our sins and make everyone that accepted him as their Lord and Savior perfect in the eyes of God. So the central question that I quibbled over and over after the death of my children: do I believe this or not? Do I accept this claim? His claim and its implications?

I have learned in 10,220 days since my daughter's death that Jesus Christ's characteristics are ones of consistency. He is the same today, tomorrow, last week, last year, and forever. It was I that lost these consistencies. When things go wrong as they always will, we tend to blame everyone except ourselves.

As it says in Galatians 6:9, "Let us not lose heart for in due time we shall reap if we do not grow weary."

I still have no idea why God does what he does or lets the things that happen the way they happen. I won't know until I come face to face with him after my death. The definition of my life had changed drastically after going through life's tragedies. My life had been wrapped up with the definition of success as being able to provide an abundant amount of financial security for my family and not give life's worries a second thought. I was wrapped up in the attitudes and thoughts that I was the only one that was affected by these tragedies. I could not understand why God was throwing these curve balls to only me. Every time I thought my life and career were headed down the road to success. I was suddenly and violently jerked into the ditch. I had to adjust my thoughts and actions. I discovered after many years that I needed to humble myself before God instead of running from him. Once I was able to move my life from me to we and include God in the we column good things seemed to happen. Attitudes, priorities, relationships, and our marriage all seemed to bring on a new light. My wife and I have always loved one another, but every marriage has their rocky times.

Once I included the big guy, everything changed for the better. What I had to learn was that my children were a lot better Christians by far then I was. They did not question God in any way. My son's attitude and perspective, while it could have been as indignant as mine, was stellar and he was a tremendous supporter of the Lord Jesus Christ. He wanted everyone to know that God was great and just even while in the situation he was going through. God sees what we can't see and understand. I couldn't see that God uses everything and every situation for his good. He must have put our family in these circumstances for a reason. I think that today my faith is stronger and wiser than any time by many degrees. You have to be flexible because our time schedule and God's time schedule are not sometimes the same. Sometimes and I should say many times, I have to ask myself are these my plans or should I make sure these are God's plans for my life? We should always remember what I totally forgot for many years, it would be well to put God as our guide.

Remember, it is his timing not ours. I do have absolute faith that my folks, my wife's folks, and my two children will be there when our time comes to show us where we are going to spend eternity. It has been a long hard road. Remember that a wound never heals completely. It only scabs over. But once we reach the scab stage, we can experience the relief from the wound bleeding all over the place. We are able to change the perspective and attitudes in our lives. This is a huge gift that God has given to us and our families. We have gotten through this journey without divorce or some other huge problem in our lives. By facing grief and talking about our feelings, we have been able to find peace with God's help. Now I can continue to work on the acceptance from God and continually ask for forgiveness from these grief-related problems that I was so ignorant about. Thanks to my beautiful wife and family and my God that my days are filled with sunshine from above.

Great-grandfather, Dr. Carr

My great-grandfather on my dad's side of the family wrote these words over a hundred years ago in his funeral messages. He received his doctorate of theology at Oxford University in England. He was a minister for over fifty years of his life and gave hundreds of sermons. I am lucky to have some of his handwritten sermons.

NUMBERS 23:10
DEATH RECOGNIZED AS THE COMMON LOT OF ALL—
NOT SO MUCH THE DYING—ME DESIRE TO BE SOR-
ROUNDED BY CHRISTIAN INFLUENCE—MEN DESIRE
TO DIE AT THE ALTER. TO DIE LIKE THE RIGHTEOUS
WE MUST LIVE LIKE THE RIGHTEOUS DEATH BED
CONVERSATIONS.

<u>Numbers 23:10</u>

Death recognized as the common lot of all — not so much the dying — men desire to die surrounded by Christian influence — men desire to die at the altar. To die like the righteous we must live like the righteous — Deathbed conversions —

CHRONICLES 29:15

OUR DAYS ON THE EARTH ARE AS A SHADOW

THE SHADOW IS A FIT EMBLEM OF HUMAN LIFE FROM
THE HOUR IT FALLS ON THE DIAL, IT MOVES AROUND
THE LITTLE CIRCLE UNTIL THE SUN SINKS WHEN IN A
OMENT IT IS GONE. A FEW HOURS PAST AND ITS WORK
IS DONE, THE SHADOW THROWN BY THE BRIGHTEST
SUNSHINE MUST VANISH WHEN THE NIGHT COMES.
SO WITH LIFE.

GOD SPEAKS TO US THROUGH NATURE WITH A PUR-
POSE. WE ARE NOT TO PONDER IN OUR HEARTS
ON THE ANALOGY BETWEEN HUMAN LIFE AND
NATURE IN ITS VARIOUS PHASES FOR PLEASURE
OF INDULGING SENTIMENTAL FEELINGS—WHEN
MOSES MUSSED ON THE BREVITY OF LIFE. HE PRAYED
"SO TEACH US TO NUMBER OUR DAYS"—LIFE IS
SHORT, SO WE MUST SEEK FOR WISDOM TO MAKE

"Our days on the earth are as a shadow."
1 Chron 29: 15.

The shadow is a fit emblem of human life. From the hour it falls on the dial, it moves round the little circle, until the sun sinks, when in a moment it is gone. A few hours past, and its work is done. The shadow thrown by the brightest sunshine must vanish when the night comes. So with life.

1. God speaks to us through nature with a purpose.

We are not to ponder in our hearts on the analogy between human life and nature in its various phases for the pleasure of indulging in sentimental feelings ———. When Moses mused on the brevity of life, he prayed, "So teach us to number our days &c." ———. Life is --- short, so we must seek for wisdom to make

THE MOST OF IT. NO MORE IS REQUIRED OF THEM THAT EVERY MAN SHOULD DO HIS BEST, WITH THE HOURS ENTRUSTED TO HIS CARE. BREVITY SHOULD LLEAD US TO VALUE TIME HIGHLY.

OUR SHORT TIME ON EARTH SHOULD BE A LIFE OF WORK, AS WE SHALL HAVE ALL ETERNITY FOR REST. LEARN TO VALUE TIME, 1ST BEAUSE YOU HAVE THE WORK YOUR "HANDSS" FIND TO ACCOMPLISH—2ND BECAUSE YOU HAVE TO "TO WORK OUT YOUR OWN SALVATION." THE GREAT LESSON WHICH THE FRAILTY AND BREAVITY OF LIFE SHOULD TEACH US IS, THE IMPORTANCE OF PREPARING FOR THE ETERNITY BEYOND.—

the most of it. No more is required
than that every man should do his
best with the hours entrusted to his care.
2. Life's brevity should lead us to value
time highly.
Our short time on earth should be a
life of work, as we shall have all eternity for rest. Learn to value time,
1st because you have the work your "hands
find" to accomplish — 2nd because
you have to "work out your own
salvation". The great lesson which
the frailty and brevity of life
should teach us is, the importance
of preparing for the eternity
beyond. —

ABOUT THE AUTHOR

Mike Newton is a happily married husband, father of six beautiful children, one son and five daughters, and a grandfather to thirteen wonderful grandchildren. Born into a family of five, he was the middle child. He grew up in a small community in Central South Dakota. Self-employed for over fifty years. He and his wife Donna Jean owned a successful insurance agency touching thousands of lives. He was a school board member, city council member, mayor, and bank board director for several years.

Mike was baptized into the Christian faith, later ordained as elder, and has given sermons in several churches. Mike finished college to become a teacher but only did that for a year before going into business for himself. Mike and his wife and sometimes his family have been able to travel the world to over forty foreign countries and across the entire United States, including Alaska and Hawaii. He always believed traveling was a great educational opportunity for his family and himself. He became disgruntled with life when he lost two children, a near death of a granddaughter, a grandson born with seizures, and the loss of two friend's wives through murder by their husbands. He lost faith in God for several years and decided to put his feelings and emotions in print, hoping to help others to know that God is always with you. Now Mike is always willing to help others whenever there is a need.

CPSIA information can be obtained
at www.ICGtesting.com
Printed in the USA
BVHW05s0615170518
516411BV00024B/251/P